WRITING TO LEARN

WRITING
TO LEARN

WILLIAM ZINSSER

PERENNIAL LIBRARY

Harper & Row, Publishers, New York
Cambridge, Philadelphia, San Francisco, London
Mexico City, São Paulo, Singapore, Sydney

A hardcover edition of this book was published in 1988 by Harper & Row, Publishers.

First PERENNIAL LIBRARY edition published 1989.

Library of Congress Cataloging-in-Publication Data

Zinsser, William Knowlton.
  Writing to learn.

  "Perennial Library."
  Bibliography: p.
  Includes index.
  1. English language—Rhetoric—Study and teaching.
2. Interdisciplinary approach in education.   I. Title.
PE1404.Z56   1989   808'.042'07   87-45825
ISBN 0-06-272040-6 (pbk.)   92 93 RRD 10 9 8 7 6 5 4 3 2 1

Contents

Contents

Preface

I wrote this book to try to ease two fears that American education seems to inflict on all of us in some form. One is the fear of writing. Most people have to do some kind of writing just to get through the day—a memo, a report, a letter—and would almost rather die than do it. The other is the fear of subjects we don't think we have an aptitude for. Students with a bent for the humanities are terrified of science and mathematics, and students with an aptitude for science and mathematics are terrified of the humanities—all those subjects like English and philosophy and the arts that can't be pinned down with numbers or formulas. I now think that these fears are largely unnecessary burdens to lug through life.

This book is a personal journey in which I confronted some of my own fears and lived to tell the tale. What started me on it was my interest in the trend in American schools and colleges called "writing across the curriculum," whereby writing is no longer the sole possession of the English teacher but is an organic part of how every subject is taught. It's an idea I like very much. It establishes at an early age the fact that writing is a form of thinking, whatever the subject. It also makes writing more appealing by enabling students to write about subjects that interest them and that they're good at. The chemistry student who freezes at the mention of Shakespeare or Shelley can write surprisingly well about how oxidation causes rust—or could if anyone asked him to.

Up to now most teachers haven't thought of such subjects as being reachable through writing or as having any kind of literature. But every discipline has a literature—a body of good writing that students and teachers can use as a model; writing is learned mainly by imitation. Therefore I decided to look for the literature myself: to collect brief examples of good, accessible writing in a variety of academic disciplines. My hope was to demystify writing for the science types and to demystify science for the humanities types.

One condition I set was to stick close to the formal discipline. I wouldn't look for writing, for instance, by journalists, good though it might be. If the discipline was geology I wanted good writing by a geologist. If it was evolution I wanted Darwin, if it was relativity I wanted Einstein, if it was cell biology I wanted Lewis Thomas. I wanted to show that it's not necessary to be a "writer" to write well. Clear writing is the logical arrangement of thought; a scientist who thinks clearly can write as well as the best writer. My book, in short, would be mainly an anthology—a guided tour of good writing in different crannies of the B.A. curriculum.

But something happened when I actually started to write. The book took on a life of its own and told me how it wanted to be written. I found myself yanked back to many corners of my past—to long-forgotten people and projects and travels that together taught me much of what I know. I realized that my life had been a broad education and that I couldn't write a book about learning without saying how much it has meant to me to be a generalist in a land that prefers narrow expertise. The anthology began to look suspiciously like a memoir.

I didn't fight the current. On the contrary, the writing of the book proved one of its central points: that we write to find out what we know and what we want to say. I thought of how often as a writer I had made clear to myself some subject I had previously known nothing about by just putting one sentence after another—by reasoning my way in sequential steps to its meaning. I thought of how often the act of writing even the simplest document—a letter, for instance—had clarified my half-formed ideas. Writing and thinking and learning were the same process.

The light bulb that went on over my head at this discovery told me what my book was *really* about. I saw that "writing across the curriculum" wasn't just a method of getting students to write who were afraid of writing. It was also a method of getting students to learn who were afraid of learning. I was once such a student, morbidly afraid of the sciences and other disciplines that looked alien and forbidding. Now I began to think that I could have written and thereby reasoned my way into those disciplines—far enough, at least, so that they would have lost their terrors.

The only thing I didn't understand was exactly how this would work. How would someone, for instance, write chemistry, or physics, or geology? My journey led me to professors in different parts of the country who told me. Well, then, how about mathematics? Surely *that* couldn't be written. Surely it could. Joan Countryman (Chapter 9) cured even my math anxiety. This is a book full of born teachers.

But above all it's a book full of ideas—other people's ideas— and what I'd like most is for readers to just enjoy those people and those ideas. Nothing about the book is definitive. I've left out many disciplines that other writers might have put in; my purpose is to suggest possible approaches, not to touch every base. Similarly, my examples of good writing are just one man's choices—passages I happened to know about or happened to discover during my trip. One of the pleasures of writing the book, in fact, was not knowing who I would meet.

Once I met them, however, there was no mistaking the men

and women I wanted to have along on the ride. They all had
the rare gift of enthusiasm. Again and again I was struck by the
exuberance that these writers brought to what they were writing about. Whoever the writer and whatever the subject—the
biologist Rachel Carson writing about life on the ocean floor,
the anthropologist Clifford Geertz writing about a cockfight in
Bali, the art historian A. Hyatt Mayor writing about the litho-
graphs of Toulouse-Lautrec, the zoologist Archie Carr writing
about the giant sea turtle, the psychiatrist Robert Coles writing
about the gallantry of children under stress, the naturalist John
Muir writing about an earthquake in Yosemite Valley, the composer Roger Sessions writing about Beethoven and the mystery
of composition—the common thread is a sense of high enjoyment, zest and wonder. Perhaps, both in learning to write and
in writing to learn, they are the only ingredients that really
matter.

New York
April, 1988

PART I

1. Hermes and the Periodic Table

As a boy I spent four years at a boarding school in Massachusetts called Deerfield Academy that had two legends attached to it. The first was its headmaster, Frank L. Boyden. When he was a young man just out of college, in 1902, he accepted a position that only a teacher desperate for a first job might have taken: running a moribund academy in the tiny village of Deerfield. The school had so few boys that the new headmaster had to play on the football and baseball teams himself. By the time I got there, in the mid-1930s, Frank Boyden had built Deerfield into one of the best secondary schools in the country, and when he retired, in 1968, his place in American education secure, he had been headmaster for sixty-six years. During all those years he also coached the football, basketball and baseball teams, continuing as an octogenarian to rap out sharp grounders for infield practice before every game. His favorite baseball strategy was the squeeze play—a mark, perhaps, of his Yankee practicality. He was an unusually small man with a plain New England face, slicked-down black hair, and metal-rimmed glasses; nobody would have noticed him in a crowd or picked him out as a leader. But three generations of boys were shaped for life by his values, and I was one of them.

The second legend was his wife, Helen Childs Boyden. A tall, bony woman with a face even plainer than her husband's, she

wore her black hair tied in a bun and she peered out at the
world through thick glasses, triumphing over eyesight so bad
that it would have immobilized a person of weaker will. Helen
Childs had also come to Deerfield as a young teacher, fresh out
of Smith College with a science degree. She married Frank
Boyden in 1907 and for more than sixty years was a strengthen-
ing presence in his life and in the life of the school. She was best
known, however, for her senior course in chemistry. The legend was that she could teach chemistry to anybody. As it turned
out, she couldn't teach it to me.

The fault was undoubtedly mine. I'm sure I didn't want to
learn chemistry. Probably I had also persuaded myself that I
couldn't learn chemistry, or any of the hard sciences. Those
subjects were for all those people who had an aptitude for
them—the ones who carried a slide rule and could take a radio
apart. I was a liberal arts snob, illiterate about the physical
world I lived in, incurious about how things worked. The
courses I felt most comfortable with were English and languages, and in my extracurricular hours I indulged my other
two loves—playing baseball and writing for the school newspaper. I did what came easiest and avoided what I might not be
able to do well.

My favorite language was Latin. It transported me back to the
classical world, and yet it was anything but dead—thousands of
its roots were alive and well in English; in fact, no subject has
been more useful to me as a writer and an editor. I took Latin
for three years at Deerfield until there were no more courses
left to take, finally getting beyond Caesar's dreary wars and
Cicero's prim orations to Virgil's *Aeneid* and Horace's odes,
finally discovering that the wonderful language also had a wonderful literature.

My teacher in that liberating third year was a man so vener-
able that he seemed to be a schoolmaster from the nineteenth
century. Recalling him now, I think of pictures of Darwin as an

old man. Charles Huntington Smith had silky white hair, a white mustache and a white goatee, and he wore the black suit and high collar befitting his age and dignity. But his eyes were young, and so were his passions for what he taught. He had turned his classroom into a small corner of ancient Rome. Large framed photographs of the Forum and the Colosseum hung on the walls, and he had also sent away for plaster reproductions of some of the great statues of antiquity. Hermes on tiptoe, beckoning the gods, was on his desk, and the Winged Victory was nearby, still sending her message about beauty and line across the centuries. Mr. Smith was obviously aware of the power exerted by the icons that inhabit the classrooms of our childhood; when I was in Italy during World War II, the first time I got a few days off I hitchhiked to Rome to see the Forum, though the distance was great and the hours I could spend there were short.

In my senior year reality caught up with me: I had to take Mrs. Boyden's chemistry. I remember her classroom almost as vividly as Mr. Smith's. I can still smell its acrid smells, alien to my humanist nose. I can still see the retorts and beakers and other strangely shaped vessels designed for measuring whatever they were designed to measure. But the icon that dominates my memory is the huge chart of the periodic table of the elements that hung at the front of the room. Those cryptic letters and numbers, so neatly arranged in their boxes and columns, were the Hermes and Venus of the chemistry class—the gods whose laws and whims would rule our lives. Each box contained its own tremendous story of natural forces working out an ordained pattern. What could that story possibly be? I never found out. The periodic table continues to rebuke me for my indolence.

Mrs. Boyden had devised a teaching method that I remember as slightly cute but that obviously worked for three generations of boys. It had something to do with one molecule joining hands with another and going off to form a different combination. I must have resisted these little romances, for by about April someone in authority began to think the unthinkable: I would flunk the college entrance exam in chemistry. This would not only ruin my chances of getting into Princeton; it would besmirch Deerfield's proud record of placing its seniors in America's best colleges.

The solution was for me to take the Latin exam instead. I was released from Mrs. Boyden's charge and told to cram for Latin. The decision was easier made than executed; after a year the intricate carpentry of Virgil's language—the capricious declensions and conjugations, the gerunds and gerundives and the dreaded ablative absolute—had slipped away and had to be hastily stuffed back into my brain. The exam was almost as hard to pass as chemistry would have been. But I was rescued by memory and by an instinct for how languages work and was duly admitted to Princeton.

There I continued to skirt the courses that would have made me a more broadly educated man. I satisfied the science requirement by taking biology, which didn't hold the terrors of chemistry and physics; any boob can dissect a dogfish. Besides, the dogfish and I had many systems in common. Poking about in its innards, I at least knew what I was looking for: heart and lungs and a digestive tract. Unlike the molecule, they could be seen and touched and examined.

On December 7 of my sophomore year, Pearl Harbor ended our reverie of life as an orderly succession of events. Our first impulse was to rush out and enlist, but we were told that "Washington" wanted us to stay in college and get educated for "the war effort." So began the age of "acceleration" at Princeton. Through the winter, spring and summer of 1942 we took courses that were compressed and elided. Our education had the quality of a speeded-up movie; we became part junior before we finished being sophomores and never knew how many credits we were amassing. The main thing was that we were amassing wisdom, which Washington in its own wisdom would harness to smash the Axis. Meanwhile several gruff men on the gymnastics and physical education staff, whom I had naturally never seen before, labored with ill-concealed contempt to build our muscles. Washington wanted us to be tough.

By fall the texture of college life began to unravel. So many professors and students had slipped away that nobody knew who was still around. At the end of the term I also left and enlisted in the army. By then I was more senior than junior, my credits badly tangled. But it could all be straightened out when I came back.

My next three credits I earned just by putting on a uniform. Princeton decided that time spent in the service was time educationally spent, and in my case that was true. My love of remote travel was born on the morning after my troopship landed in Morocco; I awoke to a landscape so startlingly beautiful and exotic—my first glimpse of the Arab world—that I've never forgotten the impact of the moment. We were informed of Princeton's decision about the extra credits in one of the letters that President Dodds periodically wrote to all of us who had gone off to war—letters that caught up with us in places where we had never expected to be. One of them reached me in a sand-blown tent near the Algerian town of Blida, and it enclosed a complete list of Modern Library titles. The university would like to send us three books, President Dodds wrote; we should just check our choices. I did, and my three books reached me six months later in a snow-blown tent near the Italian city of Brindisi.

When the war in Europe ended, in May of 1945, the troopships taking men home were assigned to France and England; the Mediterranean theater would have to wait. In July, however, I heard that the army was establishing a college in Florence to keep at least some of its soldiers occupied. Eager for more credits, whatever odd form they might take, I applied and was allowed to attend. Our campus was an aeronautical academy that Mussolini had built in his best Fascist style.

I knew nothing about art, so I decided to take art history courses. It was the ideal time and place—Florence had just begun to bring back the statues and paintings that had been hidden during the war. Crowds of Florentines gathered to watch these installations, as they had when the works were new; it was a re-Renaissance. For me it was the best of summers. On weekends I hitchhiked to other Tuscan towns that were almost as rich: Pisa, Lucca, San Gimignano and my favorite of them all, Siena. When the summer was over I received three certificates saying that I had passed three courses. But only I knew how much they certified.

In November a huge troopship finally came and took us home. Disgorged into civilian life, I needed to know whether my army credits would give me enough units to graduate. If not, I would have to go back to Princeton for one more term. When I had left I was sure I would want to return. Now I only wanted to be given my degree and to get started on whatever I was going to do next.

My hopes were not high, however, on the morning when I went to Princeton for an interview with the official who would judge my case. The certificates that I was clutching—the pieces of paper so gratifyingly won in Florence—now looked crude, wholly lacking in academic authority. I went into Nassau Hall and was told that my appointment was with Dean Root. Dean Root! I might as well turn around and go back to New York.

Robert K. Root, who was then in his seventies, was dean of the Princeton faculty. I had never met him, but I had taken his sophomore course in English literature and listened week after week to his lectures. They were stern disquisitions, raining on our unappreciative heads the fruits of lifelong scholarship, excavating with dry precision the buried ironies of Swift and the unsuspected jests of Pope, which even then I continued not to suspect. My only other view of Dean Root was at the head of the procession that commenced the service every Sunday morning in Princeton's chapel. Gray and solemn, bowed under robes representing the highest honors of Academia, he seemed to belong to Oxford or Edinburgh, not to brash young America. Surely such a man, guardian of Princeton's virtue, would scorn the grab bag of credits I now emptied at his feet.

Dean Root studied my Princeton transcript gravely. Then he studied my certificates and said he had never seen anything like them. Next he began adding up my credits. I could tell that he didn't know how much weight to give my army learning. I could also tell that he wasn't optimistic. I remembered that he had a habit of chewing the inside of his cheek, and now his mouth was working rapidly. He shook his head and mumbled that I seemed to be a little short of the necessary total.

Then, imperceptibly, the arid dean disappeared and I was talking with a person. He asked me what I had done in the army, and where I had gone, and what I had thought about. I could hardly believe that it was the same Dean Root. Was this the face that had cowed three generations of students since he had been hired as a young instructor by an earlier president of Princeton, Woodrow Wilson? I found myself talking to him with enthusiasm, describing my travels in North Africa and my trips to Rome and my Renaissance summer in Florence and my visits to Siena and the other Tuscan towns. By then I was sure that I didn't have enough credits and that the official part of my interview was over. Not until later did I realize that this was the only part that mattered to Dean Root.

At the end a look of sadness came into Dean Root's eyes and he said, "Tell me—I suppose Siena was mostly destroyed during the war?" I realized that I was the first messenger to come back from Tuscany. Suddenly I understood what Siena would mean to this quintessential humanist; probably Dean Root had first

visited Siena as a young man himself. Suddenly it was possible
to understand that Dean Root had once been a young man. I
told him that Siena hadn't been touched by the war and that the
great striped cathedral was still there.

Dean Root smiled fleetingly and saw me to the door. He said
the university would inform me of its decision soon. Not long
afterward he wrote to tell me I had met Princeton's require-
ments for a degree and would be given my diploma at a special
graduation for returning servicemen early in 1946. I've always
suspected that he waived one or two credits to make my total
come out right. I've also thought that if Siena had been destroyed I would have had to go back for another term.

But one thing I'm sure of: My education really began that day
in Nassau Hall. Dean Root freed me to get on with my life.
Learning, he seemed to be saying, takes a multitude of forms;
expect to find them in places where you least expect them to
be.

In January I rented a cap and gown and received my dubious
B.A. and went out into the world. Several months later I got a
job with the *New York Herald Tribune* and began what has
turned out to be a career of trying to write clearly and—as an
editor and a teacher—to help other people to write clearly. I've
become a clarity nut. I've also become a logic nut. I'm far less
preoccupied than I once was with individual words and their
picturesque roots and origins and with the various fights over
which new ones should be admitted into the language. Those
are mere skirmishes at the edge of the battlefield; I will no
longer man the ramparts to hurl back such barbarians as "hopefully."

What does preoccupy me is the plain declarative sentence.
How have we managed to hide it from so much of the population? Far too many Americans are prevented from doing useful
work because they never learned to express themselves. Contrary to general belief, writing isn't something that only "writ-

ers" do; writing is a basic skill for getting through life. Yet most American adults are terrified of the prospect—ask a middle-aged engineer to write a report and you'll see something close to panic. Writing, however, isn't a special language that belongs to English teachers and a few other sensitive souls who have a "gift for words." Writing is thinking on paper. Anyone who thinks clearly should be able to write clearly—about any subject at all.

How, you might ask, do I know that—I who so diligently avoided all the courses I thought I was too dumb to understand or was too lazy to grapple with? I know it because my work has been the education I avoided. Over the years I've written or edited hundreds of articles on subjects I had never previously thought about. No other job could have exposed me to so many areas of knowledge. I've not only met a wide variety of interesting people doing things that astonished and delighted me. I've found that their ideas were never so specialized that I couldn't grasp them by writing about them or by editing someone else's writing about them: by breaking the ideas down into logical units, called sentences, and putting one sentence after another. Along the way I've also discovered that knowledge is not as compartmented as I thought it was. It's not a hundred different rooms inhabited by strangers; it's all one house. Hermes and the periodic table are equally its household gods, and writing is the key that opens the door.

That's what this book is about.

2. Writing Across the Curriculum

One spring day in 1985 I got a telephone call from a professor named Thomas Gover at Gustavus Adolphus College, a small liberal arts college of Lutheran origins in St. Peter, Minnesota. He wanted to tell me about a new program at his college tha he thought would interest me. It did. In fact, it's what got me thinking about this book.

He said that in the fall term Gustavus Adolphus would launch a curriculum in which seventy-five courses, covering the entire spectrum of a baccalaureate education, would be listed with a "W," meaning that writing would be a required part of the course, that it would be a factor in the student's grade, and that the teachers would work with the students on the process of organizing, writing and rewriting their papers and reports. Three "W" courses would be required for graduation.

The call crystallized an idea I realized I felt strongly about: that the teaching of writing should no longer be left just to English teachers but should be made an organic part of every subject. The idea, which goes by the name of "writing across the curriculum," has been very much in the air among educators for at least a decade. But I had never heard of any school or college actually trying it. (I've since heard of many.) That's why the call from Minnesota excited me. It was a chance to see the idea in action and to find out whether it was as important a trend as I thought it was.

Professor Gover asked if I would like to come out to Gustavus Adolphus and talk to the students about writing. I said I would like to come out and talk to the professors; they were the real heroes of the mission. How were they going to undertake a kind of teaching they had never tried before? How were they going to adapt writing to their discipline? How did they think writing would help their students to learn?

I asked Thomas Gover how to get to Gustavus Adolphus. He said that if I flew to Minneapolis he would meet me at the airport. I said I'd see him there.

*

As baggage I would be taking along a number of strong opinions on why so many Americans don't learn to write and why they live in so much fear of trying.

One of them has to do with English teachers. Under the American system, they are the people who teach our children to write. If they don't, nobody will. They do it with dedication, and I hope they'll be rewarded, if not here on earth, at least in heaven, for there's almost no pedagogical task harder and more tiring than teaching somebody to write. But there are all kinds of reasons why English teachers ought to get some relief. One is that they shouldn't have to assume the whole responsibility for imparting a skill that's basic to every area of life. That should be everybody's job. That's citizenship.

Another reason is that it's not what most English teachers want to do. Their real subject is literature—not how to write, but how to read: how to extract meaning from a written text. That's what they were primarily hired to teach and what they were trained to teach. Inevitably, much of the writing that English teachers assign is based on literature—on what somebody else has already written—and therefore has little reality. And what students in turn write for the English teacher is more florid than what they would write for anybody else. They reach for a "literary" style that they think the teacher wants and that they assume is "good English." But this style is no part of who they are. Nor is it necessarily good English; much of what academics write and read is fuzzy and verbose. Students should be learning a strong and unpretentious prose that will carry their thoughts about the world they live in.

Another powerful element in learning to write is motivation. Motivation is crucial to writing—students will write far more willingly if they write about subjects that interest them and that they have an aptitude for. But they don't often get that chance; writing tends to be assigned only in subjects like English or history that are identified with writing.

What also gets imparted in those classes is fear. The fear of writing is planted in countless people at an early age—often, ironically, by English teachers, who make science-minded kids feel stupid for not being "good at words," just as science teachers make people like me feel stupid for not being good at science. Whichever our type, the loss of confidence stays with us for the rest of our lives.

Much of this fear could be eased if writing became a component of how these subjects are taught. A science-minded student, if he were encouraged to write about a scientific or technological subject, would soon find that he could do it. He would discover that writing is primarily an exercise in logic and that words are just tools designed to do a specific job. Similarly, the sciences could be demystified for liberal arts types like me. We could write our way into at least a partial understanding of many subjects whose language of numbers and symbols has scared us away.

The hard part, as in swimming, is to take the plunge. The water looks so cold. Can it be warmed up? I think it can. The way to begin is with imitation.

We all need models, whatever art or craft we're trying to learn. Bach needed a model; Picasso needed a model; they didn't spring full-blown as Bach and Picasso. This is especially true of writers. Writing is learned by imitation. I learned to write mainly by reading writers who were doing the kind of writing I wanted to do and by trying to figure out how they did it. S. J. Perelman told me that when he was starting out he could have been arrested for imitating Ring Lardner. Woody Allen could have been arrested for imitating S. J. Perelman. And who hasn't tried to imitate Woody Allen?

Students often feel guilty about modeling their writing on someone else's writing. They think it's unethical—which is commendable. Or they're afraid they'll lose their own identity. The point, however, is that we eventually move beyond our models; we take what we need and then we shed those skins and become who we are supposed to become. But nobody will write well unless he gets into his ear and into his metabolism a sense of how the language works and what it can be made to do. That's a fundamental premise of this book.

Another is that the essence of writing is rewriting. Very few writers say on their first try exactly what they want to say. Recently I got a form letter from my cable TV company saying, "Next month we will upgrade our phones, so it will be difficult to reach us." A few days later I saw an interoffice memo from a supervisor requesting "a list of all employees broken down by sex." Meaning is remarkably elusive. After a lifetime of writing I still revise every sentence many times and still worry that I haven't caught every ambiguity; I don't want anyone to have to read a sentence of mine twice to find out what it means. If you think you can dash something off and have it come out right, the people you're trying to reach are almost surely in trouble. H. L. Mencken said that "0.8 percent of the human race is capable of writing something that is instantly understandable." He may have been a little high. Beware of dashing. "Effortless" articles that look as if they were dashed off are the result of strenuous effort. A piece of writing must be viewed as a constantly evolving organism.

Curiously, this hasn't been the prevailing theory in our schools. American children have long been taught to visualize a composition as a finished edifice, its topic sentences all in place, its spelling correct, its appearance tidy. Only lately has there been an important shift. The shift—in the terminology of the trade—is from "product" to "process." It puts the emphasis where it should have been all along: on the successive rewritings and rethinkings that mold an act of writing into the best possible form. If the process is sound, the product will take care of itself.

Finally, in the national furor over "why Johnny can't write," let's not forget to ask why Johnny also can't learn. The two are connected. Writing organizes and clarifies our thoughts. Writing is how we think our way into a subject and make it our own. Writing enables us to find out what we know—and what we don't know—about whatever we're trying to learn. Putting an idea into written words is like defrosting the windshield: The idea, so vague out there in the murk, slowly begins to gather itself into a sensible shape. Whatever we write—a memo, a letter, a note to the baby-sitter—all of us know this moment of finding out what we really want to say by trying in writing to say it.

This was the aspect of "writing across the curriculum" that excited me most of all. It was an idea based on two principles: learning to write and writing to learn.

*

St. Peter, Minnesota (pop. 9,000), is two hours south of Minneapolis, near the Iowa border, and Professor Gover drove me through flat and fertile country, its farms farther and farther apart. I wasn't surprised that I was bound for a college that I had never heard of and that was in such an isolated place. In my travels I've found that the teaching of writing is taken more seriously at little-known colleges and universities than at the big and famous ones. Again and again, on campuses in Kentucky and Idaho and Indiana and Missouri and other states far from the Ivy League, I've met teachers deeply committed to the task of getting students to write well. The news out there is good.

Professor Gover explained that he had been chairman of the committee that was putting writing into—and across—the curriculum at Gustavus Adolphus. I asked him how the idea took root.

"Over the years," he said, "our faculty did a lot of good-natured berating of the English department: 'Why can't you teach these students to write?' The English teachers said, 'They write well for us, but in your classes they don't have that expectation—students don't think of writing as being any part of your courses.' Of course that was true, and what it stemmed from was a lifelong sense of inadequacy on our part. Those of us who teach science and other technical subjects have always felt insecure about writing. It's not that we felt stupid—we knew that we could deal well with ideas and that we understood our discipline. But somehow when it came to putting words on paper it never came out right, and we heard about it, usually from our grade school or high school English teacher. It's like the math anxiety you see in people who don't have a bent for mathematics.

"What we found developing at Gustavus Adolphus was a sense that we should all be sharing the responsibility for teaching writing. We formed a writing committee that consisted of professors from many different disciplines, and we invited proposals for 'W' courses from the entire faculty. The response was instantaneous. As soon as the ownership of writing by the English department was lost, people in other fields said, 'I'd be willing to give it a try.' The procedure is that they have to submit a proposal and the writing committee has to approve it. To help them we're bringing in outside experts to give workshops in how to teach writing. One reason for the high response

is that everything is voluntary. If the program had been im-
posed by the administration I don't think it would work."

I asked Professor Gover what his own discipline was. He said
he was a professor of chemistry. Chemistry! A whiff of sulfur
from Mrs. Boyden's class flew in the car window. Of all subjects,
why did that have to be the one he was a professor of? Surely
there was no way to write about chemistry. I asked him how he
would adapt writing to his subject. He said he was going to
teach a course called "Chemical Discoveries That Changed the
World" and get his students to write papers about them. I liked
the title of the course and the idea of changing the world. I
asked him what some of the discoveries were.

"One was the synthesizing of urea by a German chemist
named Friedrich Wöhler in 1828," he said. "It was the first time
man had made an organic compound, which had always been
considered God's work, and the discovery touched off intense
debates about theology and philosophy all across Europe for
many years. It shook the foundations of faith."

Of course I didn't even know what urea was. Professor Gover
told me it was the chief solid component of urine. I also didn't
know that urine had a solid component. But what I did suddenly
know was that this was a chemical achievement that went far
beyond the chemistry lab.

Another discovery that Professor Gover said he would include was the formulation of the periodic table of the elements.
I asked him what there was to discover; didn't the elements
already exist? They existed, he said, but there was no organized
way of thinking about them or knowing about their affinities to
one other. He told me about the Russian chemist D. I. Mendeleyev, who noticed that certain properties of the elements
recurred periodically when he arranged them according to
their atomic number. From that observation, in 1869, he proposed the periodic law—one of the cornerstones of modern

chemistry—and devised the famous chart that puts elements with similar properties in easily identified groups and alignments.

As Professor Gover described how Mendeleyev juggled the elements into a coherent system, leaving blanks for elements that hadn't yet been discovered but whose properties he could predict, the periodic table which had intimidated me at Deerfield took on the excitement of a puzzle and a chase. If Mrs. Boyden had asked me to write a paper about Mendeleyev's search for order in the elemental soup, or about the spiritual agony that Wöhler caused by playing God, I might have been drawn into the history and romance of the subject and lost some of my fear. Now, listening to Thomas Gover's tales of Wöhler and Mendeleyev and other chemists who journeyed into the unknown, I thought, "What an interesting subject!"—no small thought for someone with chemistry anxiety. Then I thought: Probably every subject is interesting if an avenue into it can be found that has humanity and that an ordinary person can follow. Writing was such an avenue—perhaps, in fact, the main route.

*

Actually I was far readier to think this thought than I would have been ten or fifteen years earlier. The difference was that many scientists have recently begun to write about their fields in language that is not only clear but often eloquent. One of them is the biologist Lewis Thomas, whose books, *Lives of a Cell* and *The Medusa and the Snail,* vividly proved that a scientist can also be a humanist. Another is the paleontologist Stephen Jay Gould. In his monthly column in *Natural History* magazine and in books like *The Panda's Thumb* I've found myself caught up in the riddles of evolution and the miracles of the natural world. Gould never forgets one of nature's oldest laws: that everybody loves a story. Every month he tells me a remarkable story and then tells me why he thinks it came out the way it did.

Another scientist-writer is Paul Davies, author of *The Edge of Infinity,* whose latest book announced by the boldness of its title, *God and the New Physics,* that it would jump into spiritual waters where men of science have seldom deigned to go. As Davies says in his introduction, the new physicists have "had to learn to approach their subject in totally unexpected and novel ways that seemed to turn common sense on its head and find closer accord with mysticism than materialism. The fruits of this revolution are only now starting to be plucked by philosophers and theologians [and are] even finding sympathy with psychologists and sociologists, especially those who advocate a holistic approach." Davies's book opens almost as many cans of worms for philosophers and theologians as Wöhler did with his synthesized urea.

Thomas and Gould and Davies belong to a new breed of scientists who don't consider it demeaning to write for the layman and who will even admit that science doesn't know all the answers. That this historic gap between science and the humanities was closing I first noticed after I went to work for the Book-of-the-Month Club in 1979—another chapter in my continuing education. At that time the Club's members were still united in their dread of science; they would only take a science book if it came cloaked in romance (archaeology) or adventure (Thor Heyerdahl's *Kon-Tiki*) or some other humanistic garb. As long as science was disguised as a colorful yarn—grave robbers in the Valley of the Kings, explorers on rafts retracing the Polynesian migrations—readers didn't have to tax their liberal arts brain.

But in the early 1980s a new generation of readers came of age who didn't want to be coddled. Educated by the ecology movement and threatened by nuclear technology, they were eager to know more about chemistry and physics to protect themselves and their habitat. The result is that today there's hardly a subject so cerebral or abstruse, from quantum mechanics to quarks, that Book-of-the-Month Club members won't give it a try. One of their favorite writers is Douglas R. Hofstadter, whose ten-year-old *Gödel, Escher, Bach* shows few signs of fatigue. Several years ago the Club, not even blinking at the title, offered his *Metamagical Themas: Questing for the Essence of Mind and Pattern,* which ponders such imponderables as the nature of human creativity and the limits of artificial intelligence.

Impressed by those brain signals from its science-minded members, the Club sent them a questionnaire in 1986 to find out what their primary field of interest was. It listed twenty fields and asked them to choose only one. They wrote back and said they couldn't. What they were saying was that although they are scientifically inclined, they are generalists, as interested in astronomy and mathematics and evolution as they are in physics and the genetic code and the processes of life.

Watching this trend, I realized that people are no longer so imprisoned by the notion that some subjects are "too hard." Even I was less fearful; because of writers like Lewis Thomas I've begun to feel a little less dumb. But it's also a little late. I would rather have started getting smart earlier, and that's what I'd like for everybody else—a long acquaintance with the major branches of learning.

By "major branches" I mean a far broader kaleidoscope than I've been talking about here. I've singled out the humanities and the sciences because they are regarded as natural opposites, even natural enemies. But this is oversimplifying to make a point. Between English at one end of the spectrum and chemistry at the other are many subjects, like economics, that are a mystery to both camps. Some people would say that economics is also a mystery to the economists. But none of us would deny

that economics has a tighter grip on our daily lives than English
or chemistry. Shouldn't we know more about its theories and
applications? And how about all those other subjects: anthropology, engineering, mathematics, philosophy, political science,
psychology, religion, sociology? What can they tell us about how
we behave, build, think, govern ourselves and grope for values
to live by?

They can tell us as much as we want to know. Probably no
subject is too hard if people take the trouble to think and write
and read clearly. Maybe, in fact, it's time to redefine the "three
R's"—they should be reading, 'riting and reasoning. Together
they add up to learning. It's by writing about a subject we're
trying to learn that we reason our way to what it means. Reasoning is a lost skill of the children of the TV generation, with their
famously short attention span. Writing can help them get it
back.

*

One thing I like about driving into a small college town is that
I almost always know where I'll find the college: on high
ground. If the town has a hill of any kind, that's where the
founders chose to build, as if to proclaim through topography
that learning is an elevated pursuit. Gustavus Adolphus was a
Lutheran version of that ideal. Behind the short and resolutely
flat Main Street of St. Peter, with its feed stores and savings
associations, the side streets sloped upward for four or five
blocks and at the summit I caught a glimpse of the clock tower
on what I knew would turn out to be a stately mid-nineteenth-
century stone building with a name like Old North. The educational verities were intact.

At the college I spent two days talking with professors who
would be teaching "W" courses in the fall. Their disciplines
covered the gamut of a liberal education—everything from art
history and computer science and engineering to ethics and

philosophy and theater. All of them were excited at the prospect of making writing a component of their course. But they still didn't quite know how they were going to do it. We discussed possible approaches, and I mentioned how strongly I believe that writers learn by imitation. I asked the professors if they knew any examples of what they considered good writing in their field. They all did. A professor of mathematics said she knew of many elegant proofs. Two physics professors said that Einstein's theory of relativity was a marvel of lucid exposition. Other professors recalled other models they admired.

I urged them to make copies of those models for their students. Writing, I reminded them, can't be taught or learned in a vacuum. We must say to students in every area of knowledge: "This is how other people have written about this subject. Read it; study it; think about it. You can do it too." In many subjects, students don't even know that a literature exists—that mathematics, for instance, consists of more than right and wrong answers, that physics consists of more than right or wrong lab reports.

I wondered if it would be possible to go in search of the literature: to collect models of good, clear writing in different fields and put them in a book. The book would be an informal guided tour for teachers and students required to write about subjects they had never thought of writing about before. At the very least it would take some of the fear out of the writing and learning process. I also thought it would demonstrate that however disparate the fields, the same principles of good writing would apply to them all. Well-written chemistry would be achieved with the same tools as well-written art history.

All that remained was to write my book. I told the professors at Gustavus Adolphus that I would come back at the end of the fall term and see how they had made out.

3. A Liberal Education

I didn't know where my search for the literature would end, but I had no trouble deciding where it should begin. My thoughts went back to the period of my life that had been the most broadly educational of all—the decade I spent at Yale. Two jobs that I held there put me in touch with the community of knowledge at its most liberal.

My reason for moving to Yale in 1970 was to teach nonfiction writing. I had never seen Yale before and knew nothing of its traditions except that the bulldog was its mascot and the Whiffenpoofs sang at a place called Mory's, possibly on the tables. I was a fourth-generation New Yorker and had never lived anywhere else. That's also where I had had my career: thirteen years as an editor and a writer with the *New York Herald Tribune* and eleven more as a free-lance writer. Those last eleven years, working alone at home, made me desperate for human contact. Whatever Yale had to offer, I was ready.

Hardly had I unpacked my bags and my children when I got a call from the chairman of the board of the *Yale Alumni Magazine*. A sudden domestic crisis, he said, had left the magazine without an editor. He explained that the magazine had a circulation of more than 100,000 and that it went to all the alumni of Yale College and its nine graduate schools, which included schools of art, architecture, divinity, drama, forestry and environmental studies, law, medicine, music and nursing. Would I like to be the editor?

At first I thought it was an absurd thing for a middle-aged Princeton man to do. But luckily I had a second thought: What quicker way to get to know a great university? Editors are licensed to be curious. Besides, I enjoyed editing more than writing. I liked thinking of story ideas; I liked working with writers and helping them to present their writing at its strongest, and I especially liked the element of surprise: Every day an editor learns something new. I signed up for the job and did it for seven years.

I never stopped to ask, "Who is the typical Yale alumnus? Who am I editing for?" One of my principles is that there is no typical anybody; every reader is different. I edit for myself and I write for myself. I assume that if I consider something interesting or funny, a certain number of other people will too. If they don't, they have two inalienable rights—they can fire the editor and they can stop reading the writer. Meanwhile I draw on two sources of energy that I commend to anyone trying to survive in this vulnerable craft: confidence and ego. If you don't have confidence in what you're doing you might as well not do it.

As editor of Yale's magazine I took the whole university as my domain. I wanted to know what was new in every discipline and what scholars were up to in every cranny of the campus. Yale seemed to have no end, for instance, of collections that were unique: silver and textiles, Babylonian tablets and Tibetan sacred texts, Boswell papers and Franklin papers, manuscripts of Charles Lindbergh and Gertrude Stein. In 1972 I noticed that the Western History Association would be holding its annual meeting in New Haven. Why New Haven? It turned out that one of Yale's professors, Howard R. Lamar, was an eminent Western scholar. I asked him for an article explaining why the Western historians, who had never met east of the Mississippi before, were coming East now.

"In the 1940s Yale filed a claim to much of the history of the trans-Mississippi West," he wrote, "by acquiring the libraries— books, maps, manuscripts, newspapers and paintings—of six great collectors of Western Americana. Put together under one roof, they have made [Yale's] Beinecke Library a rendezvous for students of the West and prompted a course on the history of the West that I have been teaching for twenty-one years." But what most excited Professor Lamar was how "the field of Western history has taken on new dimensions and totally new meanings for the student and the public. The Old West, romantic and heroic, has in two decades become the area that epitomizes the most basic questions facing America today." His article went on to describe how some of the most entrenched American attitudes—toward Indians, toward Mexican-Americans, toward Western heroes, toward the role of pioneer women and families, toward nature and land and water—had changed almost overnight. That was news to me; my clock was still set to John Wayne and Billy the Kid.

Or—to go from land to spirit—here's a piece that originated in the Yale Divinity School. I noticed that the school had on its faculty a Benedictine monk named Aidan Kavanagh, who was a professor of liturgics. Could he explain what a professor of liturgics did? His article met my question head-on in this wonderful paragraph:

No one can teach wisdom, least of all I. But what I can do in my own field of liturgical scholarship is to engage my students in an environment of facts, method and perspective in which wisdom may be learned by us all. In this regard my peculiar field is rich. What we study, ultimately, is not texts but the ways in which people from time out of mind have regularly come together to express those values that they have found to serve them best in their own struggle to survive. I shall never live forever if I cannot make it through tomorrow morning. The strategic end is born in the tactics with which it is pursued. Little things like salt, smells, oil, bread and wine, singing and seed, dancing, laughter and tears, bodies and babies, and even thoughts and words form the tactical fabric of survival with which a liturgical scholar must deal.

On another occasion I arranged for an interview with Bert Waterman, Yale's highly respected wrestling coach. He mentioned that one of his wrestlers, Michael Poliakoff, was a classics major who was writing his senior thesis on combative sport in the ancient world; during his summer vacation he had toured the museums of England, Italy and Greece to look for classical Greek vase paintings that matched the descriptions of sport he had encountered in his classical reading. How could I get so lucky as an editor? I asked Mike Poliakoff about his search. "I chose this topic," he said, "because it's a significant gap in our knowledge of antiquity, though these sports, especially wrestling, permeated every aspect of Greek life." He showed me some photographs he had taken of vases, cups, coins and sculptures, made between 550 B.C. and 430 B.C., which depicted wrestlers and referees in positions that haven't changed since. We made a layout to accompany the interview and he wrote the captions. This was one of them:

A black-figure neck amphora of the Leagros group of Attic pottery, 520-510 B.C. The triumph of civilization over barbarism is represented as Hercules, with utmost skill and grace, defeats the giant Antaeus while the goddess Athena and the god Hermes oversee the contest. Hercules is using a "front chancery," a move popular on the Yale wrestling team today.

Those are just three articles recalled at random from several hundred that popped up in various corners of the university. Most of them were about teaching and learning and research;

many were about culture, the arts, libraries and special collections; quite a few were about sports, student attitudes and social
change. But all of them delighted me with their unexpectedness and their information. They also taught me a lesson about
the integration of knowledge: Separate disciplines are seldom
separate. Beyond that, I confirmed what I had always believed
about my craft—that there's no subject that can't be made
accessible in good English with careful writing and editing.

*

My education quickened in 1973 when I was appointed master of Branford College, one of Yale's twelve undergraduate
residential colleges. Every college has a resident master, who
presides over its life as an academic and social community.
More than a hundred Fellows are also affiliated with each college—professors, deans, research scientists, librarians and other
scholars drawn from every discipline and graduate school. One
whom I recall with particular affection was the late Aleksis
Rannit, an Estonian poet widely honored in Europe. As a postwar emigré in the United States he had become a librarian and
was now curator of the Yale's rich Slavic and East European
collections. I once asked him if he would talk at one of the
weekly master's teas that I held to expose students to people I
admired whom they wouldn't ordinarily meet. I wanted him to
talk about his past and to read some of his poems.

I still remember that afternoon for three reasons. One was
the broad humanistic canvas of his life in prewar Europe. He
seemed to have known every artist and writer who was working
on some frontier of creativity. (The painter Georges Braque was
a typical frontiersman.) I also remember that when I asked him
to conclude the afternoon by reading from a volume of his
poems, he stood up. Homage to the poem; the rest had been
mere reminiscence. But what I remember most was the beauty
of the poetry itself. Estonian is a tonal language with an unusual

structure of extended beats, and none of us had ever heard it before. But it needed no translating; if Aleksis announced that the next poem was about a lake in winter, we saw the dead leaves on the ice and felt the chill. We were in the presence of a miracle: the ability of poetry to transcend the language it's written in. The words became music and carried the same kind of emotional weight.

But the Fellow who most nourished me with the inclusiveness of his mind was Willie Ruff, professor of music and of Afro-American studies. A black jazz bassist and French-horn player, Ruff also lived in Branford College and thrived on the ideas that circulated there. One Fellow whose research interested him was Dr. Gilbert H. Glaser, professor of neurology at the Yale School of Medicine and an authority on epilepsy. Ruff had long wanted to know more about rhythm than he knew from the lifelong practice of his art, and he thought Dr. Glaser might lead him to some answers. He proposed that Branford College originate and cosponsor with the Yale School of Medicine and the Yale School of Music a three-day symposium at which "the best minds in other disciplines would talk about how rhythm is at work in what they do."

I liked the idea, and so did all the people Ruff invited. (Most of them were from Yale.) Some were artists who knew rhythm through the act of creation and could demonstrate it: the jazz drummer Jo Jones, the dancer Geoffrey Holder, the poet John Hollander, some members of a Javanese gamelan orchestra, the harpsichordist and Bach scholar Ralph Kirkpatrick. But the people who gave the seminar its rigor were from disciplines that had nothing to do with performance. The metallurgist Cyril Smith talked about symmetry and dissymmetry in molecular structure. The geologist John Rodgers talked about the strict numerical repetition in the formation of crystals. The zoologist G. Evelyn Hutchinson talked about the rhythmic movement of lake waters; the art historian Malcolm

Cormack talked about rhythm in painting, and Dr. Glaser talked about the role of the brain in the physiology and control of rhythm. For three days the rhythmologists turned each other on, and Ruff has used the format ever since to teach an interdisciplinary seminar on rhythm. He keeps finding new rhythmical affinities between seemingly unrelated areas of life and inducing Yale professors—of architecture, of astronomy, of physics—to talk about them.

After I left Yale I kept in touch with Ruff and was rewarded with two of the richest experiences of my life—one in Shanghai, the other in Venice. Not only were they extensions of what I had learned at Yale about the links between widely separated centuries and cultures. They also stretched me as a writer, posing unusually hard problems when I went along on both trips and wrote articles about them that later ran in *The New Yorker.* One of the underestimated tasks in nonfiction writing is to impose narrative shape on an unwieldy mass of material. That task is so central to this book that I'll briefly describe what Ruff got me into.

The first trip took place in June of 1981. Ruff had spent two years learning Mandarin, his eighth language, in order to introduce jazz to China with the pianist Dwike Mitchell, his longtime partner in the Mitchell-Ruff Duo. The emotional climax of the trip was a concert the two men gave at the Shanghai Conservatory of Music. It began with Ruff explaining in Chinese to three hundred students and professors how jazz originated in the drum languages of West Africa—an oral tradition that was the antithesis of their own tradition—and it ended with Mitchell doing an elegant improvisation on a Chinese piece that one of the students had just performed on the piano. I could hardly believe how many opposite forces were at play in one room. But at the end music was the only force; it had blown every difference away.

Two years later I happened to call Ruff and he mentioned

that he was about to go to Venice to play Gregorian chants on his French horn in St. Mark's cathedral at night when nobody else was there. He said it was a dream that went back thirty years to his student days at Yale, when his professor was the composer Paul Hindemith. Hindemith was obsessed by the relationship between music and science—his hero was the astronomer Johannes Kepler—and he was particularly excited by the music that came out of St. Mark's basilica in the 1500s and 1600s, when Venice was the center of the musical world. The church's remarkable acoustics inspired many composers—notably, the Gabrielis, Zarlino and Monteverdi—to create an important new style of polyphonic music.

"Hindemith showed us that that music was a crucial bridge to everything that followed," Ruff said. "It was also the music that spoke most directly to me. I loved the luxurious sound that the Gabrielis achieved in their polychoral compositions, which were played and sung antiphonally from opposite lofts in St. Mark's. Ever since then I've wanted to know what that sound is like."

As for why he wanted to play Gregorian chants, Ruff said it went back to a concert that the singer Paul Robeson once gave at Carnegie Hall. To show that the folk music of many disparate countries has a common source, Robeson sang an East African tribal chant, a thirteenth-century Slovakian plain chant and an American Negro spiritual that were almost identical. Robeson explained that the Abyssinian church and the church of the Sudan were once part of the Eastern church of Byzantium. Thus African music found its way into the Byzantine liturgy, which later filtered out into Europe and colored the Gregorian chants of the early Roman Catholic Church. "So what I'll be playing in St. Mark's," Ruff told me, "is sacred music that has been played in that church since the Middle Ages. And because those chants are also at the core of my spirituals I'm going to play some of them, too."

Such a convergence of ancient streams was something I
didn't want to miss, and I asked Ruff if I could meet him in
Venice. He said he didn't know if he could get the necessary
permission; he needed to play when St. Mark's was empty so
that he could test its acoustics and make a tape recording. I said
I'd take my chances—betting on Ruff is a no-risk proposition. As
it turned out, getting permission was a story in itself—a miniser-
ies of ecclesiastical rebuffs. But finally Ruff persuaded (in Italian)
an old monsignor to let him use St. Mark's for two hours after
the last mass adjourned at seven-thirty.

Even now I find it hard to believe that those two hours happened to me. In summer, St. Mark's is visited by twenty-five
thousand tourists a day. But on that night, except for the sacristan who let us in, Ruff and I were the only people there. The
first note that Ruff blew on his French horn told us that Hindemith had been right—the note seemed to seek out every
crevice in the five immense domes and to linger long after it
should have died away. Ruff opened a book called the *Liber
Usualis* and began to play some of the oldest chants in the
Catholic liturgy: Glorias and Kyries from various masses, a Sanc-
tus, an Agnus Dei, and the beautiful "Pange Lingua." The
sound was extraordinarily pure.

I sat in the nave and watched the daylight ebb out of the
church. Suddenly the gold mosaics in the domes were drained
of color and the interior was dark. The sacristan came and put
a candle next to Ruff's book. Ruff kept playing. He and I were
alone with our thoughts—a thousand years had been collapsed
into two hours. I was listening to music that had been played in
St. Mark's since it opened in 1067.

Outside in the square, a clock struck nine. Ruff closed his
Liber Usualis and stood under the central dome and played
"Were You There When They Crucified My Lord?" The great
Negro spiritual sounded as majestic as the Gregorian chants.

When Ruff finished, the sacristan came hurrying from wherever he had been. *"Bene! Bene!"* he said, clapping his hands, trying to convey his joy, though his face said it all. That the American spiritual moved him more than the chants of his own Catholic liturgy was the final mystery of the night, although, finally, it was no mystery; all the spirituals that Ruff played, including the pentatonic "Go Down, Moses," were so similar to what he had played earlier that I could hardly tell which was which. Not that I was in any mood to try.

Back in New York, trying to write my article, I felt overwhelmed (as I had with the Shanghai piece) by the richness of the material. The story had no end of connections between different centuries and civilizations, including a visit to Stravinsky's grave. Too much had been thrown at me, and I would need to throw quite a lot at the reader. It's not enough for a nonfiction writer to just write good, clean sentences; he must organize those sentences into a coherent shape, taking the reader on a complicated trip—often with several flashbacks— without losing him or boring him. In this case a reader couldn't begin to accompany Ruff on his rounds—intellectually or emotionally—without knowing something about Hindemith and the acoustics of St. Mark's, about the Gabrielis and the Venetian school, about the Byzantine liturgy and the Gregorian chants and the Negro spirituals with which they share a distant ancestry. But too many facts would kill the reader's enjoyment of the adventure itself, which, beneath all its layers, was just an old-fashioned story of a pilgrim on a quest.

Whenever I embark on a story so overloaded with good material I despair of ever getting to the end—of covering all the ground I know I'll need to cover to tell the story right. In my gloom it helps me to remember two things. One is that writing is linear and sequential. If sentence B logically follows sentence A, and if sentence C logically follows sentence B, I'll eventually

get to sentence Z. I also try to remember that the reader should
be given only as much information as he needs and not one
word more. Anything else is a self-indulgence. Prior knowledge
of the subject, incidentally, isn't a requirement; only the ability
to arrange information in narrative order. Readers may well
have thought I was an expert on the Venetian school of music.
In fact I had never heard of the Venetian school of music or the
Gabrielis until Ruff told me he was going to Venice, and I didn't
learn any other details until I flew there and met him at a café
overlooking the Grand Canal. The trip was instant education—
sufficient, at least, to enable me to tell my story to other generalists like myself.

After that came the hard part: wrestling my new-found education into a narrative that moved logically from A to Z. The
only thing I knew at the beginning was how I wanted the article
to end: "The sacristan unbolted the door and gave us a warm
Italian goodbye and we stepped out into the crowded streets of
Venice." But every preceding sentence was slow labor: the
steady accretion of detail and the equally steady removal of
whatever I had put in that I realized wasn't doing necessary
work or that the reader could figure out for himself. (I had
learned by long travail a far from obvious lesson: Readers must
be given room to bring their own emotions to a piece so
crammed with emotional content; the writer must tenaciously
resist explaining why the material is so moving.) Only when the
job was over did I enjoy it. I don't like to write, but I take great
pleasure in having written—in having finally made an arrangement that has a certain inevitability, like the solution to a mathematical problem. Perhaps in no other line of work is delayed
gratification so delayed.

So much for the acoustics of St. Mark's and the carpentry of
writing. I've told the story because this is a book about process:
the process of transmitting information clearly and simply.
Only by repeated applications of process—writing and rewrit-

ing and pruning and shaping—can we hammer out a clear and simple product.

*

Now, as I began to think about my book, I thought of my years at Yale and all the teachers there, like Willie Ruff, who took me into their special worlds. I especially remembered Yale professors who cared about good writing even though their subject wasn't English.

The first ones who came to mind were the historians; they were the writing stars of the faculty. They understood that writing is the mechanism by which a historian passes his knowledge on to the next generation, and they insisted on good writing in their students' papers before they considered whether the paper was good history. I also recalled professors in other disciplines who saw clear writing as the corollary of clear thinking—and therefore as a key to learning.

I made a list of about ten and sent them a letter. I said I was looking for brief examples—around five hundred words—of good writing in their discipline that would be accessible to someone of high school age. Had they written any such passages themselves? (I knew they had.) If not, would they recommend a passage that some other scholar had written? The response was swift and generous. Envelopes containing photocopies of admired passages began to come back in the mail, and the accompanying letters often steered me to writers I hadn't known about or raised points I hadn't thought about. Edmund S. Morgan, for instance, my favorite stylist among the history professors, wrote:

"I find I am hard put to pick a passage of five hundred words, because the passages I like best usually depend on the preparation of the reader in earlier passages that give resonance to things said later. Indeed the quality I call resonance is what hits me hardest in all writing. And what resounds is not merely things said earlier but common knowledge and experience that everyone can relate to. I'm sending you a few passages from Samuel Eliot Morison (whom I consider the best historical writer, not necessarily the best historian, of this century) and from Perry Miller and George Otto Trevelyan. I'm not sure any of them will be appropriate for you because their principal virtue is their suggestiveness (resonance), not their clarity."

Fair enough: Resonance would have to be factored into the equation. Yet I had no trouble detecting it in the brief passage that Professor Morgan sent me from one of his own books, *The Birth of the Republic,* which he diffidently included along with Morison, Miller and Trevelyan. I wasn't surprised to find that I liked it better than anything else in his package:

The government of Great Britain had not been designed to cover half the globe, and when Englishmen were not busy extending their possessions still farther, they were apt to regard the problem of turnpikes in Yorkshire as vastly more important than the enforcement of the Navigation Acts in New York. Administration of the colonies was left to the King, who turned it over to his Secretary of State for the Southern Department (whose principal business was England's relations with southern Europe). The Secretary left it pretty much to the Board of Trade and Plantations, a sort of Chamber of Commerce with purely advisory powers. The Board of Trade told the Secretary what to do; he told the royal governors; the governors told the colonists; and the colonists did what they pleased.

This system, or lack of system, had at least one virtue: it did no harm, a fact evidenced by the rolling prosperity of mother country and colonies alike. The British Empire, however inefficient in its management, was very much a going concern, and wise men on both sides of the Atlantic believed that its success was intimately connected with the bumbling way in which it was run. They saw both the prosperity and the inefficiency of the empire as results of the freedom that prevailed in it. Freedom, inefficiency, and prosperity are not infrequently found together, and it is seldom easy to distinguish between the first two. The British Empire was inefficient, but its inhabitants were prosperous, and they were free.

The passage is hard to beat for clarity—and for warmth and humanity and a leavening touch of humor. But surely it also has resonance. If resonance is the product of "common knowledge and experience that everyone can relate to," there's nobody who can't relate to the experience of government-by-bumbling—and no American who can't relate to the balancing act called American democracy, a marvel of inefficiency that has somehow never quite lost us our prosperity or our freedom.

Another professor on my list was Dr. David F. Musto, professor of psychiatry and the history of medicine at the Yale School of Medicine, one of whose special interests is the history of drug addiction in America. In 1972 he brought me an eye-opening piece for the *Yale Alumni Magazine*—at least it opened *my* eyes—which said that "the use of opiates like heroin and morphine in the United States has been so great, compared with other nations, that some American scientists around World War I called heroin or morphine addiction 'the American disease.'" Cocaine use was even more common. "From about 1880 to 1900," Musto wrote, "cocaine was a standard stimulant or tonic, and some of our most popular soda pops had cocaine in them."

To illustrate these startling facts in a layout, Dr. Musto brought me some turn-of-the-century advertisements in which pharmaceutical firms extolled the therapeutic value of their drugs. One, for instance, was for Metcalf's Coca Wine, whose active ingredient was cocaine. Two other ads proudly introduced heroin as a cough suppressant. One was run by Bayer, who later made aspirin in the same laboratory. The second ad, run by Martin H. Smith & Co., Chemists, declared: "The problem of administering heroin in proper doses in such form as will give the therapeutic virtues of this drug full sway, and will suit the palate of the most exacting adult or the most capricious child, has been solved by the pharmaceutical compound known as GLYCO-HEROIN. The results attained with Glyco-Heroin in the alleviation and cure of cough are attested by numerous clinical studies that have appeared in the medical journals within the past few years." The adult dosage was one teaspoonful every two hours, with a half-dose suggested for children over ten, and five to ten drops for children of three and older.

After that I kept track of David Musto's articles because he seemed to be a vigilante on a dimly lit frontier, where the ignorance of doctors meets the acquiescence of the sick. When I asked him for some examples of his writing, he sent me a recent piece from the *Bulletin of the New York Academy of Medicine.* It began like this:

It is a sad paradox that the healing arts can cause sickness and disease. From witch doctors and early Western medicine, down to the era of William Harvey or Benjamin Rush, the posthumous "Father of American Psychiatry," we deal with a profession which for centuries routinely inflicted grievous bodily harm without qualm and, further, often at the behest of society. Physicians confidently treated battle wounds with boiling oil and infectious diseases with blistering, vomiting and purging.

Many of these treatments lasted into our century, among them calomel, or mercurous chloride, perennially popular with physicians and the public and still prescribed in the period between the two world wars. Phlebotomy or bleeding was considered legitimate almost as long. Even Sir William Osler, the most noted physician in the English-speaking world, recommended phlebotomy for selected cases of pneumonia as late as 1909.

The medical profession has a long record of treating patients with useless or harmful remedies, often in clinical settings of complete mutual confidence. Iatrogenic diseases, complications and injury have been, in fact, common in the history of medicine. We may look upon addiction to certain dispensed drugs as one variation among the occasional effects of drug therapies.

"Iatrogenic" means "caused by medical treatment." It's a medical term with a precise meaning, and Dr. Musto was writing for a medical journal. Still, his use of the term doesn't invalidate his article as an example of clear writing for anybody. "Iatrogenic" is easy enough to look up, as I just did. Not only did I enjoy learning a new word; Webster's definition adds an ironic phrase that makes the rest of Dr. Musto's piece all the more disturbing: "said esp. of imagined symptoms, ailments or disorders induced by a physician's words or actions." Here's how his story continues:

During the 19th century, with the development of organic chemistry and the manufacturing pharmaceutical industry, the purity of natural substances improved. As the composition of natural substances such as opium and coca leaves was separated into several active ingredients, the potency of drugs increased. Further, modes of application were improved so that these active ingredients, such as morphine, could be more effectively introduced into the body's physiology. Here the most dramatic step forward was the development of the hypodermic syringe. By the second half of the 19th century several addicting forms of opium were available. . . .

Because of the enormous humanitarian value of reducing pain and fear, [opium] became a pawn in the vigorous competition for patients among health deliverers. There were more people offering health care—homeopaths, regular physicians, natural bone-setters, local wise ones and so on—than com-

munities needed. Confusion over medical theories, the abun-
dance of physicians and a growing objection by patients to the
severe treatments meted out by regular physicians—they
called it "heroic treatment"—made an opiate a very attractive
remedy: it was painless, it worked, it relieved pain and worry
and it made tolerable a host of ailments whose cause and
proper treatment were completely unknown. Small wonder
that the importation of crude opium into the United States
started to rise early in the century and grew more rapidly than
the population. In 1840, when importation statistics commenced, to the mid-1890s, when the per capita consumption
began to level off, the amount of crude opium for each person
in the United States grew from 12 grains to 52 grains.

The article goes on to document the steady march of iatrogenic addiction in this country, noting that "the most important
play of America's greatest playwright," Eugene O'Neill's *Long
Day's Journey into Night,* is "a drama of iatrogenic addiction"
and pointing out that the dangers of "physician-induced dependence" have proliferated in our own time with the mass pro-
duction of tranquilizers and other anxiety-reducing pills.
"Great temptations are held out to physicians who are able to
relieve symptoms in spite of the dangers inherent in the drugs'
multiple and often addictive effects."

Dr. Musto's article was just the kind I had hoped to find for
my book, bringing a scholar's knowledge to a complex situation
or issue. I wanted to present enough examples from enough
fields to suggest that every discipline has an accessible literature
waiting to be found by teachers and students. I wanted to elimi-
nate such excuses as "It can't be done" and "There's nothing out
there."

History and writing are of course natural allies, whether it's
colonial history or medical history; one couldn't live without the
other. But what would I get from professors in fields where

writing was a more unlikely bedfellow—geology, for instance—
or where it had rarely been allowed in bed at all? And what
about all those conveniently vague humanities? I remembered
that the late Brand Blanshard, professor of philosophy emeritus
at Yale, once gave me a small book called *On Philosophical
Style,* in which he explained how to write about that most
vaporous of subjects. Such courage doesn't come along every
day. I got out his book and took hope from this early passage:

> Hard as philosophy is, there have been writers who have
> actually succeeded in making it intelligible and even exciting,
> not to the exceptionally gifted alone, but to a wide public.
> Socrates talked it, and Plato wrote it, in a way that some
> millions of readers have not been willing to forget. Bergson,
> without once descending to vulgarity, made it for a time one
> of the excitements of Paris. The British tradition in philosophy
> has been exceptionally fertile in writers with the gift of mak-
> ing crooked things straight. So if a philosophical writer cannot
> be followed, the difficulty of his subject can be pleaded only
> in mitigation of his offense, not in condonation of it. There are
> too many expert witnesses on the other side.

So I began to cast my net for expert witnesses. But what I first
needed to know more about was how writing was related to
learning. How much do we learn about a subject through writing that we wouldn't learn in any other way? To find some of
the answers I would have to return to Gustavus Adolphus College and see how that first term of writing across the curriculum
had gone.

4. Writing to Learn

I regretted my decision to go back to Gustavus Adolphus College in January when the pilot of my plane announced that the temperature in Minneapolis was twenty-five degrees below zero. We were over Lake Michigan and I didn't see any easy way of turning back. Twenty-five below! I could *die* if my rented car broke down while I was driving across the frozen tundra of Minnesota. I was a city boy from New York; I didn't have any of the survival knowledge that Minnesotans are born with, or any of the special equipment they carry in their cars— Sterno stoves and heavy blankets and dried foods—to keep from perishing along the highway. I would just have to take my chances, and I did, hunched against the unbelievable cold, squinting at the snow-blown landscape through the icy windows of my car and guessing at the whereabouts of the road. When I finally got to Gustavus Adolphus the woman who greeted me said, "I hope you at least had a rope in your car. A few years ago six people died not far from here when a sudden blizzard came up and they got out and couldn't find their way back. You should always have a rope that you can tie to your steering column."

I had of course been ropeless, but that didn't matter now. I had survived, and the Gustavus Adolphus faculty quickly warmed me up. For two days professors from every corner of the curriculum came and talked to me. Quite a few were men and women I had met on my previous visit. I asked them how they had taught their "W" courses during the fall term and what they had discovered. Their accounts varied in detail, but on one point they all agreed: Far more learning had been achieved by the addition of a writing requirement.

Many teachers included themselves among the learners. Barbara Simpson, professor of psychology, said: "I wanted to teach a 'W' course because I write very badly myself—in high school I was terrorized by writing. One thing I did last term was to ask students to write a paper in the last five minutes of class, summarizing what I had said in my lecture. It helps them to find out whether they understood what I was talking about. Psychology is a deceptively difficult subject: It sounds like material you've known all your life, but actually it's based on extensive research. And the writing has become far more concrete. In the '60s psychology was still a probabilistic science, so it developed a hedging language. You can't get away with that today."

Fuzzy thinking turned up repeatedly as the main enemy. "Students don't know how to be precise," said Norman Walbek, associate professor of political science. "In my first assignment I asked them to write a paper on 'What are the most important goals of United States policy?' It was a values statement—something nobody had ever asked them to write before; usually students are only asked to describe or to analyze: 'Write an essay on the Declaration of Independence.' Well, their papers were a disaster. They rambled all over. They couldn't formulate a goal or a policy except in the most generalized way—'better communications,' 'world peace'—and in almost every case the comment I found myself making was: 'I don't understand this.' As the term went on I tried to get them to use writing to focus their thoughts on specific ideas and issues. I told them I'd be grading their papers for clarity, common sense, logic, plausibility and precision, not for the content of their views. At the end of the term I gave them the same assignment on goals and policies. This time their papers were clear and explicit. Their problems were in thinking, not in the mechanics of writing."

Professor Clair McRostie, who teaches International Economics and Management, didn't wait to discover this dismal fact; he knew it already. The prospectus that he handed out to his students left them in no doubt about his priorities—it said that their three required papers would be graded for "quality of writing, grammar, spelling, organization and content." His first three lectures, in fact, were devoted entirely to writing and reasoning.

"Back when some of us were concerned about why Johnny can't write," Professor McRostie told me, "a psychologist put it to us that Johnny can't reason, and I've been preoccupied with that thought ever since. The first two books I assigned last term were *The Art of Thinking*, by Vincent Ruggiero, and *Reasoning*, by Michael Scriven. This is a generation that has spent fifteen thousand hours watching television, and its attention span is short. I'm challenging my students to find their powers of reasoning. I tell them, 'If you don't write reasonably and well on your exam I'll give you a lower grade. But I'll also give you extra time if you need it.' At the end of the term, when they were asked to evaluate the course, they said that the writing component had been an important part of their learning."

I liked the audacity of a professor devoting his first three lectures to subjects that weren't the ones he was supposedly there to teach. It was a way of seizing his students' attention with a radical piece of news: Economics and management are important, but they're not as important as clear reasoning and writing; without them, all the economic theory in the world won't take you far. Professor McRostie had me beat as a logic nut, and his credentials were better. I had merely learned by experience that thinking is the foundation of writing. But I had never thought about thinking as a process. How does it work?

Why do some people think straighter than others? What are the factors that prevent us from thinking clearly? Can it be taught? I made a note to buy *The Art of Thinking* when I got back home. I suspected that it would help me to see how so much fuzz gets into the writing machinery and how some of it might be kept out.

"Reading, writing and thinking are all integrated," said Kevin Byrne, associate professor of history. "An idea can have value in itself, but its usefulness diminishes to the extent that you can't articulate it to someone else. What the writing program made *me* realize is that I have to take much more time in class to talk about writing. Teachers have a tremendous tendency to just give writing assignments and let their students sink or swim—which assumes that they've learned to write somewhere else. Very often they haven't. In history we've paid great lip service to the need to write, but we haven't taken the time in our classes to tell students how it's done. We need to rob time from the study of history to do that. It takes a commitment, and I found it very painful because the term is too short anyway to cover all the historical issues I'd like to discuss."

Early in the term Professor Byrne told his students to bring in a historical passage that they considered well written and to explain why. "It forces them to think about the elements that go into good writing," he said, "and it shows them that there are many different kinds of good writing, not just one. I was amazed at what happened when students questioned each other about the *writing* in a historical account. Their ideas became much more focused when the whole class discussed a passage in terms of how it was written."

In all these accounts I heard a pleasant sense of discovery: Writing could get into corners that other teaching tools couldn't reach. But it was a professor of chemistry, Lawrence W. Potts, who took me to the heart of what I had come to find out. During the fall, he said, he had taught a "W" course called "Instrumental Methods of Analysis" for juniors and seniors who hoped to go into chemistry as a profession.

"I've been grading my students' lab reports both for their scientific merit," Professor Potts said, "and for the language in which they tell me what they did, what their results were and how they interpret those results. If they don't write well they lose a full grade. Like all writing, it's an exercise in thinking. The easy way for a chemistry professor to evaluate lab work is just to have students turn in index cards with the numbers they got. But students don't get much out of that—there's an important link they miss.

"I want them to go first to the literature, so they know how the experiment has been done before and what to expect in the lab and how to plan their work. Having to plan their work helps them to write it up as they go along, so that writing becomes woven through the entire class and lab experience. If they fall into a pitfall they can explain how they got there, and that's education. The process also enables *me* to see how their mind worked. By having them describe how they arrived at a result I can comment on it, and they can make use of my comment when they go back to the experiment. There's a feedback that isn't possible when the teacher just grades from numerical answers. Revising helps the students to rethink."

I don't remember whether I cried "Eureka!" when I heard that. Not being Greek, I probably didn't. But I do remember thinking I would probably never get a more concise statement of what writing across the curriculum is all about, or a better illustration of how the act of writing gives the teacher a window into the brain of his student. See Johnny reason! Watch him make a wrong turn! Follow his cogitations as he wonders what to do next!

I thought of all the subjects where the teacher never gets this inside look, where students are graded solely on the basis of a right or a wrong answer. I don't only mean hard sciences, like physics, that deal in numerical answers. The humanities and the social sciences also rely heavily on tests that measure a student's learning by what he knows, not by how he got to know it: multiple-choice exams and "short-answer questions." Economics, for example, is a discipline that rests finally on numbers and projections and probabilities—"answers," as they might be loosely called. But the future economist should be as accountable as the future chemist for describing the steps that took him to his numerical result, and the economics teacher should be no less eager to read about the trip.

Eagerness to read and correct student writing, however, is not a commodity that grows on trees; it's far easier to just check right and wrong answers. Unfortunately, there's no quick and easy way to teach writing. When I first did it I assumed that a good part of the job could be accomplished by explaining in class the elements that constitute good writing. Surely if I assailed my students with my sacred principles of clarity and simplicity and brevity, if I exhorted them to use active verbs and short words and short sentences, if I pointed out the pitfalls that await the writer of a travel piece or a sports piece or an interview, they would go and do what I had told them to do.

No such transfer takes place. Writing teachers are lucky if 10 percent of what they said in class is remembered and applied. The bad habits are just too habitual. They can be cured only by that most painful of surgical procedures: operating on what the writer has actually written. Only there, where a writer is at his most vulnerable, having put some part of himself on paper, does he make the connection between principle and practice. The operation is almost as hard on the teacher. Like the parent who tells the spanked child that "this hurts me more than it hurts you," the writing teacher wants nothing so much as a paper that's well written—one that won't mire him in endless repairs and emotional debris. I sometimes find myself emitting small moans as I start to read a paper and realize the magnitude of the problems ahead.

Why, then, would anyone in his right mind want to be a

writing teacher? The answer is that writing teachers aren't altogether in their right mind. They are in one of the caring professions, no more sane in the allotment of their time and energy than the social worker or the day care worker or the nurse. Whenever I hear them talk about their work, I feel that few forms of teaching are so sacramental; the writing teacher's ministry is not just to the words but to the person who wrote the words. One of my hopes for writing across the curriculum is that teachers in many fields will discover this transaction. Through the writing of our students we are reminded of their individuality. We are reminded, whatever subject we are charged with teaching, that our ultimate charge is to produce broadly educated men and women with a sense of stewardship for the world they live in.

A funny thing happened on the way to that ideal when the first space satellite was launched by the Soviet Union in 1957. Overnight, Sputnik turned us into a nation obsessed by technology and determined to produce a bumper crop of technicians every year. Pure science has been an American deity ever since. Many science professors say that their discipline is now taught without any reference to its past traditions or to its present or future impact on society.

"I was a Sputnik student," Professor Potts told me. "I graduated from Oberlin in 1967, and the chemistry I was taught was all hard-core science. The only time you talked about values was over coffee. As a result, my generation of chemistry teachers has been afraid to get into the background of the subject because we were never exposed to it ourselves. But now colleges like ours are paying more attention to the history and the ethics of science. We're also trying harder to reach the non-science student. This term, for instance, I'm teaching a course on hazardous wastes called 'Chemical Time Bombs,' and I've asked for a paper summing up the legal and ethical issues of Love Canal. That course wouldn't have been taught ten years ago."

If such values aren't imparted in the classroom they will probably never get imparted; college students who are praised and coddled for acquiring technical knowledge aren't likely to have an onset of ethics when they get out in the world of profit and loss. Yet moral dilemmas have never been woven so bewilderingly through American life. Every day we are assaulted by scientific or biomedical questions that we don't even know how to think about, from toxic wastes and "Star Wars" and nuclear energy to acid rain and gene splicing and surrogate motherhood. Many of them are the legacy of scientists who now admit that they didn't understand how their decisions would affect the quality of life, or life itself. Too many sick chickens have come home to roost. Too many lakes and rivers have died, too many fish and birds, too many people in states like Utah who had the bad luck to live downwind from the scientists. Too many names that we had never heard before—Bhopal, Chernobyl, Three Mile Island—have become instant synonyms for technology gone wrong.

That's why I liked the two trends that Professor Potts mentioned: educating future scientists to be more attuned to the impact of their work, and educating the rest of us to be more scientifically literate. It does us no good to just feel a growing sense of jeopardy over what the scientists are "up to." As citizens we're responsible for what we know and what we don't know.

Where does writing figure in all this? Writing is a tool that enables people in every discipline to wrestle with facts and ideas. It's a physical activity, unlike reading. Writing requires us to operate some kind of mechanism—pencil, pen, typewriter, word processor—for getting our thoughts on paper. It compels us by the repeated effort of language to go after those thoughts and to organize them and present them clearly. It forces us to keep asking, "Am I saying what I want to say?" Very often the answer is "No." It's a useful piece of information.

One of the most striking things I heard at Gustavus Adolphus came from a professor of philosophy, Deane Curtin. He said, "Many of my 'A' papers last term were 'failures.' A great paper in philosophy is often one that tells me why the student couldn't get where he wanted to go. That's progress. It's better than deluding yourself that something was proved that really hadn't been."

I liked the example because I've always believed that failure is one of the great teachers, every bit as instructive as success. It's not, however, a point that Americans want to hear. Winning is the national creed. Forget the pursuit of happiness—is the kid an "achiever"? How we love the student who "tests" high. How we hate the football team that loses. Reading the letters in the *Princeton Alumni Weekly,* year after year, I marvel at how bothered this highly educated segment of the populace is by the fact that their alma mater can't field a winning football team. There is no end of ululation in the letters column.

But failure isn't the end of the world, in football or anywhere else. In writing—and therefore in learning—it's often the beginning of wisdom. The point came up again when a professor of religion, Garrett E. Paul, told me about his course in "Ethics in Business and Economics." Early in the term he assigned his students a paper that would be read aloud in class.

"It gets them to write for their peers and not for the teacher," he told me, "and what they learned was a revelation to them. They learned by the presence or absence of response to what they had written. The good paper raised all the right questions, and on those days the paper would teach the class. The poor paper was instantly noticeable. There wouldn't be much in it to discuss—there'd be no place to start, or it was so unclear that we'd have to go back over it and try to figure out what it was about. It made everybody in the class realize that a piece of writing is a piece of thinking. By the end of the term all the students said how much better they understood a subject by having to write about it."

Like his colleagues, Professor Paul had found many models of good writing in his discipline. One of his favorite assignments dealt with the issue of morality in advertising. Students were told to read a chapter on the "dependence effect" from John Kenneth Galbraith's *The Affluent Society* and then to read a rebuttal by Friedrich von Hayek, called "The Non-Sequitur of the Dependence Effect." (Both are in an anthology called *Ethical Theory in Business*.) "What I particularly pointed out," Professor Paul said, "was the elegance of von Hayek's argument. It's elegant in the sense of a geometric argument: Everything that needs to be there is there, and the essay has nothing in it that doesn't support the argument. I also emphasized to the students how short von Hayek's answer is. I'm paying much more attention now to the quality of the writing that we discuss in class."

*

So my two days at Gustavus Adolphus gave me a glimpse of most of the courses that might be encountered in a liberal education and of the role that writing could play in learning them. Some of the disciplines caught me unaware of how they had changed. A professor of geography, for instance, Robert B. Douglas, said that he now insists on writing as a major component of his classes. "I keep in touch with my recent graduates," he told me, "and they all say that what they really needed in college were writing courses, because they now have jobs in fields like urban planning or retail store location, or in agencies for economic development or rural land use planning, and they have to write a great many reports, which have to be clear."

To give his students due reverence for the mother tongue, Professor Douglas sends them to the books of his literary hero,

J. B. Jackson—books such as *The Necessity of Ruins* and *The Vernacular Landscape*. "Every review of a new book by J. B. Jackson," he said, "begins by calling attention to the clarity of his language, the brevity of his prose and the beauty of his style. I use him in two ways. I might tell a student, 'Let's see what Jackson has to say about the character of small towns in the Midwest, or about the grid plan of city streets.' Later I get them to critique the writing style itself. *Why* is it so effective?"

Hearing from so many academic provinces, I occasionally wondered: What does the English department think of all this? I got my answer from Claude C. Brew, associate professor of English.

"Writing across the curriculum reinforces what we do," he said, "and of course it gives writing a much broader base. That's a healthy direction. In this country the English major has always been defined almost entirely in terms of literature and literary analysis, and therefore English department writing has a strong literary bias. In fact, the teaching of writing has only recently been incorporated in graduate English programs. Our education as English teachers never prepared us to do that.

"I was lucky in coming to Gustavus Adolphus because the college has a tradition that everybody in the English department teaches composition. I taught one course for five years in writing about science, which opened me to criticism from my department colleagues. But I learned something important: I got horribly literary papers from my students, because they thought that's what an English teacher would want. They wrote things in those papers that they would *never* say. I tried to show them that science has a fine literature of its own. I got them reading the essays of Victor Weisskopf and books like Loren Eiseley's *The Immense Journey,* Stephen Jay Gould's *Ever Since Darwin* and Thomas Kuhn's *The Structure of Scientific Revolutions.*"

I asked Professor Brew what he thought of the "comp/lit"

double grade that many English departments use to distinguish between how a paper is written and what it says.

"I don't approve of it," he told me, "because it emphasizes the split. Writing is not divisible." I was greatly cheered to hear this truth affirmed by a professor of English. Professors of English are by no means unanimously delighted to see "their" subject—writing—parceled out to teachers beyond the tribal walls. *Chemistry* teachers! *Geography* teachers! Many English teachers would rather hold on to the keys. Why, they ask, can't they correct a chemistry paper for its writing and let the chemistry teacher correct it for its chemistry? The answer, of course, is that an act of writing is an act of thinking—an organic compound, as the chemists would say. There's little point in having a teacher clean up the messy syntax in a chemistry paper if he can't also clean up the messy chemistry. The indivisibility of language is what gives writing its authority and its majesty. Lewis Thomas writes eloquently about cell biology because in his bones he is a cell biologist. That he also happens to be a good writer is a bonus.

My last visitors at Gustavus Adolphus were two professors of nursing, Ann Garwick and Marilee Miller. Their appearance at the end of a long parade of academics took me by surprise. I was secure in my knowledge that nurses are primarily technicians and that most of them work in hospitals. What would technicians want with reading or writing or a baccalaureate education?

The two women quickly set me straight. High technology has taken over many nursing tasks in hospitals, they said, and far more nurses are now out in the world of health care, keeping watch on some of our most important frontiers. "The value of a baccalaureate education for nurses today," said Professor Miller, "is that it helps them to become leaders and decision-makers and advocates. The caring role is critical, and often nurses are the only people in a community who are in a position to see what's happening to a family when something goes wrong—for instance, when the child of two working parents gets sick—and to find a solution.

"We push our nurses to be agents of change on health issues: everything from seat belts to day care to the right of employees to know about hazardous substances in their work environment. We're trying to make our nurses more socially aware and more politically astute. One course we require them to take is 'American Minorities.' It's a sociology course that helps them to understand how to work with different cultural groups. There's a big Southeast Asian population in Minneapolis, where many of them will be based."

Both professors make their students do extensive reading and writing. "We're pushing them into the literature," Professor Garwick said. "Among other things, we ask them to make a search of the pertinent journals and then to choose one article that particularly interests them and to write an annotated summary of it. Writing helps them to organize their plan of health care. It also expands their thinking and raises further questions that they ought to be asking. It's exciting to work with our students on their successive drafts. A wonderful thing happens when they realize they don't have to write in isolation—that they have a colleague who will go over their work with them—and when a section that had been giving them trouble just falls into place on the next draft."

Listening to the two women, caught up in their enjoyment of what they were teaching, I suddenly thought it was the most natural thing in the world that they had made reading and writing an integral part of their nursing courses. How else will we get the kind of nurses we need to make a difference in a society groping for decent health care? I had known all along that I liked the idea of writing across the curriculum. But nobody had told me how far across the curriculum it could reach.

5. Crotchets and Convictions

The artist Paul Klee once told his students that "art is exactitude winged by intuition." I like that equally as a definition of good writing. One of the things I enjoy about Klee is his willingness to be surprised during the creative process by an antic idea. Paintings that might have been cold because of their exactitude are animated by humor, nonsense and whim. Klee's humanity keeps jumping out of his material; I feel connected not only to the artist but to the man, especially because so much of the nonsense makes sense.

As a writer I'm no less grateful than Klee presumably was for unexpected visitors from the subconscious mind. In this book, memory has already taken me down many roads where I hadn't expected to go. I was startled, for instance, to find that I had forgotten all about the Latin teacher who so influenced me at Deerfield; the name Charles Huntington Smith and the silky white goatee jumped out at me in their full Victorian splendor. Once again I was struck by one of the miracles of the cognitive process—that the act of writing will summon from the buried past exactly what we need exactly when we need it. Memory and intuition and chance associations will always generate a certain percentage of what any writer writes. The remainder is generated by reason.

Therefore, for the purposes of this book, I'll generalize outrageously and state that there are two kinds of writing. One is explanatory writing: writing that transmits existing information or ideas. Call it Type A writing. The other is exploratory writing: writing that enables us to discover what we want to say. Call it Type B. They are equally valid and useful.

As a teacher I've concentrated on Type A writing because it's so badly needed. We are a society paralyzed by the inability to convey routine information—the inability of the executive to explain company policy in a memo to the staff, of the employee to explain his new idea in a proposal to the boss, of the bank to explain its "simplified" new bank statement to the customer, of the manufacturer to explain in a consumer manual how its product works, of the health and insurance professions to explain in a brochure how to get reimbursed for being sick, of the educator to explain in a letter how the school is educating our children, of the Internal Revenue Service to explain on its new tax form how to fill it out. Type A writing is what most people need to get through the day, both as writers and as readers. Its sole purpose is to inform; it has no deeper content that the writer will discover in the act of writing.

My advice to Type A writers begins with one word: *Think!* Ask yourself, "What do I want to say?" Then try to say it. Then ask yourself, "Have I said it?" Put yourself in the reader's mind: Is your sentence absolutely clear to someone who knows nothing about the subject? If not, think about how to make it clear. Then rewrite it. Then think: "What do I need to say next? Will it lead logically out of what I've just written? Will it also lead logically toward where I want to go?" If it will, write the sentence. Then ask yourself, "Did it do the job I wanted it to do, with no ambiguity?" If it did, think: "*Now* what does the reader need to know?" Keep thinking and writing and rewriting. If you force yourself to think clearly you will write clearly. It's as simple as that. The hard part isn't the writing; the hard part is the thinking.

Type B writing—exploratory writing—requires no such cogi-
tation, no prior decisions about which road to take; the road will
reveal itself. Today many of America's best writing teachers
believe that this is the only kind of writing worth teaching,
especially to young children. Unlike Type A writing, which they
consider mainly a technical skill, Type B writing is a voyage of
discovery into the self. Only by going into uncharted territory,
they feel, can a writer find his potential and his voice and his
meaning. Meaning, in fact, doesn't exist until a writer goes
looking for it.

I don't entirely buy that theory because I think both types of
writing are necessary for survival and fulfillment. But I like the
humanism behind it—the idea that writing is a means of growth
and that it should never be without elements of joy and wonder.
Nor do I think Type B writers are exempt from the laws of
grammar and order. However subconsciously they may stum-
ble on what they want to say, they are finally as obligated as
every other writer to make themselves understood. "Free writing" is a search mechanism, not a license to let it all hang out.

Such theorizing, however, is too vague to be useful here. It's
time to get down to fundamentals. What makes good writing
good and bad writing bad? Here are some notions that are
important to me.

*

FICTION AND NONFICTION. This book has nothing to do
with fiction. I'm dealing only with nonfiction, or factual writing,
by which I mean all the kinds of writing that harness the world
we live in and are therefore accountable to the truth. By contrast, the fiction writer—the writer of novels and short stories—is accountable only to his art. His gift is that he can take
us into interior worlds where the fact-bound writer can't go:
worlds of imagination, rumination and fantasy. In return we
enter into a more forgiving contract with him, allowing him to

come at his subject slowly, discursively, obliquely, elliptically or just plain densely if that's his vision. Density, in fact, is one of the qualities that William Faulkner's fans most like about him.

I'm not into density; I'd make a lousy editor for Henry James—I'd cut out all the elements that make him Henry James. But I respect every novelist's right to do things his own way. I like *Catch-22, Gravity's Rainbow* and *Zen and the Art of Motorcycle Maintenance,* for instance, because the authors of those three surrealistic novels—Joseph Heller, Thomas Pynchon and Robert Pirsig—invented their own rules, knowing that the old ones wouldn't do the job they had in mind. Probably many people dislike those novels as much as I dislike Faulkner. But as readers of fiction we have no right to say that the author's method was "wrong." We can only say it didn't work for us.

No such immunity is granted the nonfiction writer. He can do all kinds of things wrong. He is endlessly accountable: to the facts, to the people he is writing about, to his "quotes," to the mood, to the ethical nuances of the story. He is also accountable to his readers. They won't put up with being delayed, lost, confused, bored or taken down unnecessary trails by failures of craft. Fiction may still be worshiped on the slopes of Parnassus as the higher form. But writing good nonfiction is in many ways harder and more exacting work.

*

INFORMATION AND NOISE.   One of the most helpful books I've read recently is *Grammatical Man: Information, Entropy, Language, and Life,* by Jeremy Campbell. It's the story of "information theory," a science that wasn't born until World War II but whose laws have governed us since the first grunt. I bought *Grammatical Man* because I had begun to think of writing across the curriculum as a vast information system, and I remembered the stir the book caused at the Book-of-the-Month Club when it was published in 1982. We offered it because several of our editors were crazy about it—which is the best possible reason.

The book is not only interesting; it's a model of linear writing, leading the reader across rocky new terrain in steps of clarity and logic. Jeremy Campbell never fails to ask: "What would a novice need to know next? How can I explain it in the way that would be easiest to grasp?"

Here's how he first tells his readers about the trip they are about to set out on, one that will take them through mechanisms of sending and receiving information as diverse as language, memory, dreams, artificial intelligence, probability theory, radar, electronics and the DNA code:

> It was not until the 1940s that information was defined as a new scientific term, and this definition was quite new, unlike any in the standard dictionaries. Yet the concept of information, by being described precisely enough to satisfy mathematicians and telecommunications engineers, became increasingly fascinating for nonscientists. The word began to recapture some of its other meanings which had fallen into disuse. The view arose of information as an active agent, something that does not just sit there passively but "informs" the material world, much as the messages of the genes instruct the machinery of the cell to build an organism, or the signals from a radio transmitter guide the intricate path of a vehicle on its journey through space.
>
> Thus information emerged as a universal principle at work in the world, giving shape to the shapeless, specifying the peculiar character of living forms and even helping to determine, by means of special codes, the patterns of human thought. In this way, information spans the disparate fields of space-age computers and classical physics, molecular biology and human communication, the evolution of language and the evolution of man.
>
> Evidently nature can no longer be seen as matter and en-

ergy alone. Nor can all her secrets be unlocked with the keys of chemistry and physics, brilliantly successful as these two branches of science have been in our century. A third component is needed for any explanation of the world that claims to be complete. To the powerful theories of chemistry and physics must be added a late arrival: a theory of information. Nature must be interpreted as matter, energy, and information.

One of the recurring themes of *Grammatical Man* is the need to protect the integrity of the message. In information parlance, the enemy is "noise"—a perfect word for all the random interferences with what man or nature is trying to say. Noise is the typographical error and the poorly designed page and the caption that doesn't quite explain what's happening in the picture. Noise is handwriting that's hard to read. Noise is distortion on the TV screen. Noise is the lapse of memory, the slip of the tongue, the wrong neuron fired by the brain—anything that brings disorder to the intended order of a message. So pervasive is noise, disorder being such a strong natural force, that nature has evolved an infinite number of backup systems for getting messages to their destination "more or less in the original form," as Campbell puts it. "In nearly all forms of communication, more messages are sent than are strictly necessary to convey the information intended by the sender."

Certainly writing is one of the main endeavors where disorder is more common than order. Murphy's Law, which says that if something can go wrong it will, applies to the average sentence almost as inexorably as a law of physics. If you want a law of physics, I can commend (thanks to *Grammatical Man*) the Second Law of Thermodynamics, which states that the tendency of energy is to decay in usefulness—a change for the worse known as entropy. I found it consoling after all these years to learn that writers are up against nothing less than the fundamental anarchy of the universe; entropy, prince of dis-

order, is sprinkling noise on everything we write. Ambiguity is
noise. Redundancy is noise. Misuse of words is noise. Vagueness
is noise. Jargon is noise. Pomposity is noise. Clutter is noise: all
those unnecessary adjectives ("ongoing progress"), all those unnecessary adverbs ("successfully avoided"), all those unnecessary prepositions draped onto verbs ("order up"), all those unnecessary phrases ("in a very real sense").

Information is your sacred product, and noise is its pollutant.
Guard the message with your life.

*

OBSCURITY. Obscurity being one of the deadly sins, anyone
might suppose that serious people would labor mightily to avoid
it in their writing. But to suppose this is to overlook another
force of nature that almost equals entropy as a drag on life's
momentum. That force is snobbery. Yes, gentle reader (as the
Victorian novelists put it when they had to deal with the darker
traits), it pains me to say that there are writers who actually
want to be obscure. Their principal habitat is Academia, though
they can be spotted without the aid of binoculars wherever
intellectuals flock. Not for them the short words and active
verbs and concrete details of ordinary speech; they believe that
a simple style is the sign of a simple mind. Actually a simple
style is the result of harder thinking and harder work than they
are willing or able to do.

The thought of a writer being deliberately unclear stirs such
hostile vibrations in my breast that I'm going to let Sir Peter
Medawar make the case for me; I can trust him not to foam at
the mouth. Medawar was an English biologist who won the
Nobel Prize for medicine in 1960. I had never heard of him
until I began asking people for examples of good science writing
and his name kept bobbing up in their replies. That struck me
as a good omen, and I bought a book of his called *Pluto's Republic.* The book takes its piquant title from a remark made by one

of Sir Peter's neighbors, who, knowing of his interest in philosophy, said, "Don't you just adore Pluto's *Republic?*" It seemed to him an apt name for the "intellectual underworld"—various misconceptions about science—that his book explores. One of its essays, "Science and Literature," has this to say about obscurity:

In the eighteenth century obscurity was regarded as a disfigurement not merely of philosophic and scientific but also of theological prose. To conceal meaning (it was reasoned) is equally to conceal lack of meaning. . . . But even in those enlightened days the appeal of obscurity was clearly recognized. Of Dryden, Johnson said that "he delighted to tread upon the brink of meaning, where light and darkness begin to mingle." Don't we all, up to a point? We all recognize a voluptuary element in the higher forms of incomprehension and a sense of deprivation when matters which have hitherto been mysterious are now made clear.

The *rhetorical* use of obscurity, however, is a vice. . . . If the text is made hard to follow because of non sequiturs, digressions, paradoxes, impressive-sounding references to Gödel, Wittgenstein and topology, "in" jokes and a general determination to keep all vulgar sensibilities at bay, then we shall have great difficulty in finding out what the author intends us to understand. We shall have to reason it out therefore, much as we reasoned out a passage in some language we didn't fully understand. In both texts some pretty strenuous reasoning may be interposed between the author's conceptions and our understanding of them, and it is strangely easy to forget that in one case the reasoning was the author's but in the other case our own. We have thus been the victims of a confidence trick.

In all territories of thought which science or philosophy can lay claim to, including those upon which literature has also a proper claim, no one who has something original or important to say will willingly run the risk of being misunderstood; people who write obscurely are either unskilled in writing or up to mischief.

Medawar's own style is worth noticing before we move on. The sentences are somewhat long, but they move persuasively and also with a certain grandeur. We're in the company of a mind that has urbanity and wit and that is likable for its dislike of humbug.

Probably the most engaging advice on obscurity comes from E. B. White, in Strunk and White's *The Elements of Style,* a book every writer should read once a year. "Although there is no substitute for merit in writing," White says, "clarity comes closest to being one. Even to a writer who is being intentionally obscure or wild of tongue we can say, 'Be obscure clearly! Be wild of tongue in a way we can understand!' "

*

VOICE AND TONE.   Not long after reading *Pluto's Republic* I bought a book by another Nobel Prize winner: *Surely You're Joking, Mr. Feynman!* by Richard N. Feynman, as told to Ralph Leighton. I not only knew that it had been on the *New York Times* best-seller list for fifteen weeks; I had also kept running into Feynman in books by scientist-writers, like Jeremy Bernstein, who revere him as one of the giants of twentieth-century theoretical physics.

The book is an autobiography, and from about page three I had no trouble believing that Feynman is one of the smartest people in the world. But that's not what he primarily wants me to believe. The subtitle of his book is "Adventures of a Curious Character," and the blurbs make much of Feynman's reputation for being "irrepressible," "uninhibited," "outrageous," "zany" and an all-around funny fellow. The result is exhausting—Henny Youngman in a lab coat.

Maybe it's not fair to compare a book that is "told," like Feynman's, with one that is written, like Medawar's. Still, both purport to be books: They are how two great scientists chose to present themselves to the reading public. Medawar knew that how we write is how we define ourselves—our style is who we are—and his style reflects a mind that is strong and supple. Feynman's mind is no less strong and supple, but his style is strenuously breezy—he wants to be the life of the party. The two words he routinely uses for his colleagues are "guy" and "fella," even when the fella is an Oppenheimer or a Fermi or a Bohr.

I don't want Feynman to be the life of the party; I want him to be the smartest scientist in the world. In talking down to me he degrades not only me but himself. I finally had to stop reading his book. I can't handle an A-plus mind expressing itself in C-minus sentences. I believe too strongly that mind and language are inseparable. If we violate our language we violate ourselves.

My guess is that Feynman was persuaded that a book by the smartest scientist in the world wouldn't sell unless he purveyed himself as the lovable fella next door, and certainly a fifteen-week run on the best-seller list is hard to argue with. Still, I think his writer and his editor did him a disservice. Long after *Surely You're Joking, Mr. Feynman!* has come and gone, books like Lewis Thomas's *Lives of a Cell* and Douglas Hofstadter's *Gödel, Escher, Bach* will still be around, their authors remembered as men of wisdom and stature. Thomas and Hofstadter aren't trying to be a pal to the reader; they're trying to write good English. They know that the English language, reverently used, will carry any load.

Moral: There are no cheap substitutes for the best.

*

BREVITY. In writing, short is usually better than long. Short words and sentences are easier for the eye and the mind to process than long ones, and an article that makes its case succinctly is the highest form of courtesy to the reader. Somehow

it never occurs to sloppy writers that they are being fundamen-
tally rude. Most pieces can be cut by 50 percent without losing
any substance.

Brevity is one sign of a well-organized mind. As evidence let
me present a letter by A. L. Rowse, the eminent Oxford don,
that ran in the *New York Times* on December 8, 1985, at the
height of the furor over an American scholar's claim that he had
discovered a "lost" poem by William Shakespeare. As proof the
American cited similar words and phrases that his computer
had found in the new poem and in the body of Shakespeare's
known works. Rowse demurred:

To the Editor:

I have been requested from several quarters to give my
opinion on the supposed discovery of a new Shakespeare
poem (front page, Nov. 24). It is utterly improbable for the
following reasons:

- It is quite unlike any poem that Shakespeare ever wrote.
- We know quite well from the early poems "A Lover's
Complaint" and "Venus and Adonis" what Shakespeare's
early style was; and this poem is utterly unlike it.
- Shakespeare was so famous in his own time that people
would not have overlooked anything of his. Quite the reverse.
They published under his name, to exploit it, poems that are
definitely known *not* to be his.

The conclusion is clear—impossible that this ordinary poem
is his. There are scores like it in manuscript collections.

Those who would *like* to think it is Shakespeare's are quite
good, conventional scholars, but academic. One needs to be a
practicing poet, and these scholars have no ear for poetry. A
computer is no judge of what is poetry.

That's the case stated in 133 words. Granted, Rowse's letter has
none of the high umbrage and malediction that make most

academic squabbles such enjoyable reading, but that's a whole other sport.

*

JARGON.   Jargon is the lingo of people in specialized fields who have infected each other with their private terminology and don't think there's any other way to say what they mean. Somewhere they forgot about the mother tongue. There's almost no subject that can't be made accessible in good English.

A few years ago I was shanghaied onto an advisory panel at a major corporation, and at our first meeting someone asked the chairman what the committee had been formed to do. He said, "It's an umbrella group that interacts synergistically to platform and leverage cultural human resources strategies companywide." That pretty much ended my interest in the committee, and when it subsequently experienced viability deprivation (went down the tubes) I was overjoyed. God was in his heaven after all. There's no place for such garbage in the working world.

But I was lucky; most Americans get that kind of junk inflicted on them year after year by their executives and managers. Here's how one of New York's biggest banks recently started—and continued for twelve pages—a memo to the staff:

> While our efforts cannot be characterized as having had a profoundly strategic horizon, the methodology utilized to identify strategy statements was not sufficiently program oriented for implementation.

No wonder so many Americans hate their jobs. Who wants to work for bosses who deal with the help in such dehumanizing language? The people writing and talking most pompously in America today are people in authority.

Here's a letter that a school superintendent sent to his teachers at the start of the new school year:

> In the spirit of collegiality with a commitment toward maximizing faculty involvement in the exploration and resolution of issues and needs confronting this Division in response to its multi-dimensional challenges, I suggest that the departments target representatives to begin the divisional identification of the issues and needs considered most relevant to determine what formats would be most convenient.

Spare me such collegial colleagues.

Jargon, of course, takes a multitude of forms. The two preceding examples are typical of the buzzwords—mostly nouns—that infest such fields as management, banking, insurance, education and government. They are words that make the insider feel important when he uses them but that don't really mean anything. What is a profoundly strategic horizon? Just what are those formats that it would be most relevant to determine? An outsider can only try to translate and hope for the best—a task made harder by the tendency of fad nouns to attach themselves to other fad nouns. Recently I sighted this brilliant cluster: "communication facilitation skills development intervention." Five nouns, but no human activity that I could visualize. I went at the problem like a code breaker. "Intervention" = "help" or "teach"; "development" + "facilitation" = "improve"; "communication skills" = "writing." Solution: a program to help kids write better.

More often jargon consists of special terms that every occupation has found it necessary to invent. Used with restraint, they aren't jargon; they are the working tools of a particular field, and if they serve a specific need we have no trouble learning new ones overnight: words like "amniocentesis" and "gentrification" and "superconductivity." The trouble arises when jargon becomes a crutch—when its users become so dependent on their private terminology that they claim they can't express themselves in any other way. Social scientists, for instance, are addicted almost beyond mortal help.

Consider these two sentences from a book by a famous sociologist. I didn't choose them as exceptions; the whole book is in this style.

> The third major component of modeling phenomena involves the utilization of symbolic representations of modeled patterns in the form of imaginal and verbal contents to guide overt performances. It is assumed that reinstatement of representational schemes provides a basis for self-instruction on how component responses must be combined and sequenced to produce new patterns of behavior.

That's either 86-proof jargon, preposterous and unnecessary, or it's one sociologist talking to another in language as clear to them both as "hop on Pop" or "see Spot run." I like to think that even those two sentences could be turned into relatively plain English, but I'll buy the sociologist's argument (the one he would surely make) that he is entitled to write in his tribal language if he is addressing other sociologists—for instance, in a journal of sociology. But any specialist who doesn't clean up his jargon when he's writing for the general population deserves to be, if not tarred, at least feathered by the mob.

*

THE ILLITERACY OF THE ELITE.   Whenever you see in the newspaper or hear someone say that writing in America has gone to the dogs, you can bet that it's the educated classes who are doing the bewailing and the uneducated classes and the

young who are being bewailed. But which of these two sentences is more illiterate:

1. The ongoing reconfiguration positions Barbara offsite to
hopefully identify growth and profitability potentials beyond
what is currently being realized.
2. Barbara will try to find out why we ain't doing better.

Number one—a corporate memo I found in my in-box last
year—is scandalous in its flatulence. Yet it's typical corporation-
speak. Number two is a little uneducated but a lot more helpful.
If clear writing is one of the foundations of a democratic society,
don't count on getting it from men and women with a college
degree. Ivy League alumni magazines are awash with letters so
grammatically squalid that they barely make sense. Clean-up
time at this toxic dump has to start at the top.

*

KILLER NOUNS.   Probably there isn't a writing teacher (including me) who hasn't assailed his students with George Orwell's rendering into modern sludge of the verse from Eccle-
siastes about the race not being to the swift. That's not going to
stop me from citing it again. The verse goes like this:

I returned and saw under the sun, that the race is not to the
swift, nor the battle to the strong, neither yet bread to the
wise, nor yet riches to men of understanding, nor yet favor to
men of skill; but time and chance happeneth to them all.

That's a wonderful sentence. The words are refreshingly short;
they instantly appeal to the eye and make us want to read them.
More important, all the nouns are working nouns: they denote
objects (bread) or activities (race, battle) or attainments (riches,

favor) or conditions of fate (time, chance) that we can relate to
our own lives.

This is how Orwell said the passage would come out in the
pompous bureaucratic language of our times:

> Objective consideration of contemporary phenomena com-
> pels the conclusion that success or failure in competitive ac-
> tivities exhibits no tendency to be commensurate with innate
> capacity, but that a considerable element of the unpredictable
> must invariably be taken into account.

That's also a wonderful sentence. Please remember that sentence: it's the enemy. Just at a glance it repels us—we don't
want to spend any time with a mind that expresses itself in such
bloated words. What makes the words so ponderous is that they
don't have any people in them; they only have concepts—"consideration," "conclusion," "capacity," "tendency." Nouns that
denote concepts are the death of vigorous writing. Good writing is specific and concrete.

Here's a more recent example: the Port Huron Statement,
which became the manifesto of the New Left and of the Students for a Democratic Society—and thus a prime document of
the counterculture—in 1960. It was drafted by Tom Hayden,
whose first version began like this:

> Every generation inherits from the past a set of problems—
> and a dominant set of insights and perspectives by which the
> problems are to be understood and, hopefully, managed.

For a manifesto, that's well above the acceptable limit in concept nouns, generalized ideas and passive verbs, and someone
told Hayden it wouldn't do. Rewriting it on the spot, he got
personal and specific and created a classic:

We are people of this generation, bred in at least modest comfort, housed now in universities, looking uncomfortably to the world we inherit.

*

LIFESAVING VERBS.   One way to take the mush out of concept nouns is to turn them into active verbs. Verbs are the strongest tools a writer is given, because they embody an action. Active verbs are stronger than passive verbs, because they propel a sentence forward. They also enable us to picture who did what, because they require a pronoun or a noun: "I," "we," "she," "you," "boy," "girl." Seeing a pronoun or a noun and an active verb together, we visualize a specific event that occurred at a specific moment. Passive verbs have no such energy or precision:

> ACTIVE: I saw the boys skating on the pond.
> PASSIVE: The boys were seen skating on the pond. [By whom? When? How often?]

In the following paragraph—from Norman Mailer's ringside account of the death of the welterweight boxer Benny Paret in the twelfth round of a championship fight with Emile Griffith in Madison Square Garden on March 25, 1962—notice the tremendous punch that active verbs deliver:

> Paret died on his feet. As he took those eighteen punches something happened to everyone who was in psychic range of the event. Some part of his death reached out to us. One felt it hover in the air. He was still standing in the ropes, trapped as he had been before, he gave some little half-smile of regret, as if he were saying, "I didn't know I was going to die just yet," and then, his head leaning back but still erect, his death came to breathe about him. He began to pass away. As he passed, so

his limbs descended beneath him, and he sank slowly to the floor. He went down more slowly than any fighter had ever gone down, he went down like a large ship which turns on end and slides second by second into its grave. As he went down, the sound of Griffith's punches echoed in the mind like a heavy ax in the distance chopping into a wet log.

Imagine that paragraph written with passive verbs and concept nouns: "A sensation of Paret's mortality was experienced by the audience. The feeling was retained as an ongoing presence in the atmosphere."

Active verbs are a writer's best friend. Not every concept noun can be turned into an active verb. But how many people are even trying?

*

VISIBLE DETAIL.   Writing is not unlike the schoolroom period called "show and tell." The writer should not only tell a story; he should try to make the reader *see* what he is writing about. As Mailer demonstrates, active verbs are ideal for this kind of work; they force us to witness an event.

But nouns are equally pictorial and helpful. I'm not talking (needless to say) about concept nouns. I mean the thousands of simple nouns, like "house" and "chair" and "earth" and "tree," that denote the objects of everyday life and the properties of the world we live in. Unlike the long concept nouns, which tend to be of Latin origin and to end in "ion," these are Anglo-Saxon words—short, blunt, homely and infinitely old. They are words that are in our bones and that resonate with emotions, whether we want them to or not. A writer who uses these nouns makes instant contact with the humanity of his reader by giving him a familiar picture.

The following 184-word sentence by Virginia Woolf, which begins an essay called "On Being Ill," runs counter to everything I've said about brevity. In fact, it's one of the longest sentences I've ever seen. But I like it. Its length is no problem because the author has her material under control from start to finish, and it stays in the mind's eye long afterward because of all its vivid and surprising nouns:

> Considering how common illness is, how tremendous the spiritual change that it brings, how astonishing, when the lights of health go down, the undiscovered countries that are then disclosed, what wastes and deserts of the soul a slight attack of influenza brings to view, what precipices and lawns sprinkled with bright flowers a little rise of temperature reveals, what ancient and obdurate oaks are uprooted in us by the act of sickness, how we go down into the pit of death and feel the waters of annihilation close above our heads and wake thinking to find ourselves in the presence of the angels and the harpers when we have a tooth out and come to the surface in the dentist's arm-chair and confuse his "Rinse the mouth—rinse the mouth" with the greeting of the Deity stooping from the floor of Heaven to welcome us—when we think of this, as we are so frequently forced to think of it, it becomes strange indeed that illness has not taken its place with love and battle and jealousy among the prime themes of literature.

*

ENJOYMENT.   Achieving a decent piece of writing is such a difficult task that it often strikes the reader as having been just that: a task. It accomplishes its purpose, and perhaps we shouldn't ask for anything more. But we do. We wish the writer had had a better time—or at least had given us that impression. Here's the opening paragraph of a recent biography of the illustrious man who was, among many other things, Great Britain's last viceroy of India. It's by Philip Ziegler and it's called, appropriately, *Mountbatten.*

Admiral of the Fleet, the Earl Mountbatten of Burma, was
a man who, for his own amusement, rarely took up any book
unless it were one of genealogy, most especially one relating
to his own forebears. During the reaches of the night in the
Viceroy's House in Delhi, when his predecessors might have
diverted themselves with the verses of Macaulay or the latest
detective story by Mrs. Christie, Mountbatten would relax
over the tapestry of his ancestry, enumerating the generations
that divided him from the Emperor Charlemagne and marvel-
ing at the intricate web of cousinship which bound him many
times over to the Wittelsbachs and the Romanoffs, the Habs-
burgs and the Hohenzollerns. His studies both gave him the
satisfaction that attends the solution of a complex jigsaw puzzle and gratified that pride in family that was one of the most
prominent of his characteristics.

What a lift that opening gives us. We're off on a trip with a
writer who savors his material, and no element in writing is
quite so contagious. My favorite statement of this idea came
from the humorist S. J. Perelman. I became a Perelman addict
at sixteen and never got cured. In 1978, near the end of his life,
I invited him to Yale to talk to my students. One of them asked
him what it took to be a humor writer. "Comic writing," he said,
"needs audacity and exuberance and gaiety—and the most important of these is audacity."

Then he said: "The reader has to believe that the writer is
feeling good."

The sentence hit with me tremendous force, especially when
he added, almost as an afterthought, "even if he isn't." I knew
that Perelman's life had had more than the usual share of days
when he wasn't feeling good—days of depression and emotional
travail. Yet for fifty years he went to his typewriter every morning and took his readers on roller coaster rides of such dizzying

swoops that they blew all our troubles away. Surely a writer having such a good time was a man without a care in the world.

Now, thinking of that feat, I realize that audacity was only part of what Perelman was talking about. He was also talking about courage. Humor is the most perilous of writing forms, full of risk; to make a vocation of brightening the reader's day is an act of continuing gallantry. He was also talking about energy. Energy is the divine spark in creative work. We know right away when we are in its presence—we can't hold Bach or Mozart down, or Picasso, or Mark Twain, or Frank Lloyd Wright, or Louise Nevelson, or Fred Astaire, or Lucille Ball, or Toscanini or Norman Mailer or Tom Wolfe. They sweep us along in the current of their life force. We seldom stop to think about the effort they made to switch it on and crank it up every morning.

But what Perelman was finally talking about was craft. Writing is a craft, and a writer is someone who goes to work every day with his tools, like the carpenter or the television repairman, no matter how he feels, and if one of the things he wants to produce by 6 P.M. is a sense of enjoyment in his writing, he must generate it by an act of will. Nobody else is going to do it for him.

*

IN SHORT. In short, these are some of my crotchets and convictions. Look for the convictions in Part II of this book, soon to begin. All the passages I've assembled there are the work of men and women who wrote with clarity, simplicity, warmth and enjoyment. In each case I've tried to explain why I think the piece is well written and why I like it. On the surface, therefore, Part II is an explicit lesson in how to write.

If it's also about writing to learn (and it is), I've left that mostly implicit, not wanting to numb you with repetition of the same obvious point. Only two chapters—9 and 11—specifically demonstrate writing as a method of learning. But all the writers represented in Part II wrote clearly because the act of writing and rewriting made them think clearly, organized their ideas, told them what they knew and what they still needed to know, and pushed them to new areas of knowledge.

It can do the same for you.

6. Earth, Sea and Sky

One of the few other adults who lived in our Gothic quadrangle when I was master of Branford College at Yale was a distinguished professor of geology, fast approaching the emeritus years, named John Rodgers. He had been a resident Fellow since 1948, and he was still there when I left, in 1979; he had seen masters come and go, mere ripples in the river of time. Being a geologist, he took a longer view than most people and was unruffled by such surface disturbances as families moving in and out of the master's house every five or six years.

But he was also a humanist. Amid the detritus of his apartment, which was cluttered with old scientific journals and papers, he had a Steinway grand piano, on which he played Bach fugues and Chopin études very beautifully with his strong geologist's fingers. Once he shyly asked if I would mind if he prepared and gave a recital in the college dining hall of the complete piano works of Scriabin. He thought it would be an instructive way—perhaps never tried in a concert before—of tracing how Scriabin explored different composing styles at different stages of his life.

The recital (I didn't mind) was a gem of both music and scholarship, for the geologist-pianist had also written graceful program notes to guide us on our trip. That part of the evening didn't surprise me; I knew that good writing was as important to John Rodgers as good geology. One year he was so maddened by a fuzzy student dissertation that he wrote and distributed to his classes a manifesto called "The Rules of Bad Writing." These were a few of its entries:

- Never use the same word twice for the same idea. Thus you make sure that the reader never knows whether it's the same idea or not.
- Never use the first person where you can use ambiguous phrases like "the writer" (especially when you've just mentioned some other writer) or, better still, "it is thought" or "it is considered," so that the reader can't be exactly sure who thinks what, or what—if anything—you do think.
- Never use an active verb where a passive verb will do. It pads out the sentence nicely and puts more distance between you and the facts—and the reader.

Every June, when the Yale college year was over, I knew I could expect a formal call some evening from John Rodgers—as formal, at any rate, as a call can be when the visitor is wearing mountain boots and the host is wearing sneakers. He had the punctilio of an old-fashioned don and wouldn't think of leaving for the summer without letting me know. It was the only time I felt that I was living in a novel by C. P. Snow; otherwise the life of a college master had a way of slipping imperceptibly between the ceremonial and the janitorial.

"Where are you off to?" I would say when he sat down.

"I'm going to the Urals," he would say. "I've never done the Urals. I didn't want to go until I had learned Russian." The previous summer it had been a range in western Australia. He was a man who collected mountain ranges; they were like old friends to him, as distinctive as stamps or coins or cats or any other collectible.

Now I called and asked him whether he had done any writing

about mountain ranges. He said he had written articles only for scientific journals. I told him that was good enough for me; I had a feeling that even in a scientific paper John Rodgers could make his subject clear to anybody. He sent me an article called "The Life History of a Mountain Range—The Appalachians." It began like this:

> I strongly suspect that my interest in the subject I am to discuss here was awakened when as a schoolboy I picked up in a second-hand bookshop a copy of James Geikie's book: *Mountains, Their Origin, Growth and Decay* (1913). I read it through fascinated, though of course not comprehending half of it, and despite disparaging remarks from members of my family, who dubbed it *Mountains, Their Cause and Cure,* I have been fascinated by the subject ever since.
>
> Mountain ranges are of course not living organisms, but we geologists have long believed with Geikie that they go through a sequence of stages over geologic time, from a period when nothing hints that a range will develop in the future, through a stage of origin (the geosyncline) and a period in which mountains grow (the orogeny), to a stage of decay ending in their dissection and obliteration, often in their interment beneath a cover of younger sediment. Here I shall not attempt a generic description of a life applicable to all mountain ranges, but rather a specific one, that of the range best known to me, the Appalachians of eastern North America, and at first I shall concentrate on their northern half, especially New England, beside which I grew up (reading Geikie's book) and in which I have spent the largest part of my own life history.

Could we ask for a more humane beginning? It brushes aside our apprehension that this is a discipline too dry and distant for us to comprehend. Another one of John Rodgers's articles, "The Geological History of Connecticut," written for a journal of Yale's Peabody Museum, began like this:

Geology is the science of the earth, and what particularly characterizes it is the sense of the length of the time the earth has existed. Geologists think of the long history of the earth in terms of millions of years (units of 10^6 years), just as astronomers think of immense interstellar distances in terms of light years (units of 10^{13} kilometers), and they find it convenient to divide that history into broad divisions called eras. Indeed the divisions they use are curiously like those used by historians to describe European history and can reasonably be translated as Modern, Medieval and Ancient times, plus Prehistory. (Actually they are defined in terms of the *life* of the times, for the relative ages of rock strata are determined principally by the fossil remains of life that they contain.) Even the proportions are not too dissimilar; as in history, each older era is longer than the next younger, and the oldest, the prehistory, dwarfs all the others in duration, although least is known about it. Connecticut, as we know it today, is the result of processes taking place through all these millions of years, and it preserves at least some record of each of the eras.

The process that produced the features we see in the Connecticut landscape today are processes still operating on the surface of the earth. I will pass by the plant cover—forests, pastures, lawns—and the animal inhabitants, and also man and his works, although he has already notably modified the landscape. The chief inorganic process that has shaped the hills and valleys as we see them is the work of water, especially running water, washing away the soil—eroding it—as it still does in big storm-floods, and of soil water, gradually seeping into the solid rocks beneath and converting them—weathering them, we say—into clay, mud and loam by reacting chemically with them or breaking them down physically, as when it freezes in their cracks.

The two kinds of water work together; the soil water weakens the rocks and converts them into loose material that the running water can easily wash away, and the running water carries away the debris so prepared and thus makes it possible for the soil water to penetrate still deeper. They work unevenly; some rocks are more resistant to weathering and to erosion than others, although none are completely immune, and the resistant rocks therefore remain as hills or mountains rising above the lower lands where the rocks are weaker, like East Rock and West Rock in New Haven, the Hanging Hills of Meriden, or Talcott Mountain west of Hartford.

I like the thoughtfulness that gives me East Rock and West Rock—two framing landmarks for anyone who has ever lived in New Haven—in the midst of the scientific explanation of what caused them. No science writer should be "above" pointing to anything that relates his knowledge to our lives. Professor Rodgers continues in the next paragraph to orient his Connecticut readers:

The running water runs downhill, of course, and gathers itself into watercourses, creeks and rivers, bigger and bigger downstream. Because its power to erode and especially to transport debris increases rapidly with the velocity and volume, the watercourses become valleys, and the rivers can even cut gorges through ridges of resistant rock, as the Farmington has cut through Talcott Mountain at Tariffville and the Connecticut through the highland east and southeast of Middletown on its way to Long Island Sound.

Cenozoic or Modern time has lasted about 60 million years so far, and water has been able to weather, erode and transport a great deal of rock; during that time probably some hundreds of meters of rock has been stripped off the surface of Connecticut. The eroded material has all been transported out into the Atlantic Ocean, where it has accumulated and is still accumulating on the continental shelf and off the conti-

nental edge. Thus the shapes we see in our present landscape
are all the result of this ceaseless erosion; in Connecticut we
have no mountains or other landforms built up by recent volcanic activity or uplifted along earthquake faults, such as one
finds in some parts of the western United States. As the Atlantic Ocean has been there throughout the Cenozoic era, the
land surface of Connecticut is adjusted to its presence; the
major rivers flow south or southeast, and overall the surface of
the landscape slopes in the same direction, though of course
highly varied in detail.

How easily Professor Rodgers carries us along with his narrative, sounding erudite but not professorial, luring us into his vast
time frame so painlessly that we hardly blink at the words "so
far" in the statement that Cenozoic time "has lasted about 60
million years so far," or at the "recent" volcanic activity that has
given the western United States some of its contours but has
spared Connecticut. What makes his writing work, of course, is
that it's well written. The English is clean, the order logical, the
various steps illustrated with processes that we can visualize:
the running of water, the washing away of soil. True, we visualize in infinitely speeded-up motion what it took nature millions
of years to accomplish, but the feat is that we have been enabled
to visualize it at all. This is the gift that good science writing can
bestow in all those disciplines where the scale is so unfathomably large, like astronomy, or so unfathomably small, like cell
biology and sub-atomic physics, that we can only imagine what
is being described. Language is our rope ladder across the abyss.
   One scientist who manages to simplify these immensities for
me is James Trefil, a professor of physics and author (speaking
of invisible phenomena) of the popular *From Atoms to Quarks*.
To a physicist, Trefil says, "the entire world is a physics laboratory; everything we see around us operates according to a very
small number of basic principles. There are Newton's three

laws that describe the motion of material objects, the three laws
of thermodynamics that describe things related to heat, four of
Maxwell's equations that describe electricity and magnetism,
the single principle of general relativity that describes gravity,
and a few more laws (depending on which philosopher of science you talk to) for quantum mechanics, the physics of the
sub-atomic world."

Armed with these dozen-odd laws and what appears to be a
magnetic attraction to the Beartooth range of the Montana
Rockies, Trefil has written a book called *Meditations at 10,000
Feet: A Scientist in the Mountains,* in which he muses on such
down-to-earth questions as the age of the ground he is hiking
on, noting that "the appearance of a rock, like the appearance
of a person, tells you something about the sort of life it has had."

Estimating the age of the earth has long been a major intellectual pastime of the learned. In the seventeenth century the
Anglo-Irish bishop James Ussher, by counting up the lives in
biblical genealogy, concluded that the earth had been created
on Tuesday, October 26, 4004 B.C., at nine o'clock in the morning. Later scientists used the saltiness of the ocean, the heat
flow through the earth's crust, and the rate of formation of
sediments in rivers to estimate the same number. Insofar as
one can identify historical themes in such widely diverse fields
of study, the trend throughout the nineteenth and early twentieth century was to assign longer and longer lifespans to our
planet.

With the advent of radiometric dating, an important new
tool was added to the equipment of those seeking to date the
earth. The new technique depends on a simple premise: the
earth must be at least as old as the oldest rock on its surface.
If we can find a rock that is of any datable age, we can be sure
that the earth must be older than that age.

By 1931, at a meeting of the National Research Council in

Washington, D.C., the American geologist Arthur Holmes was able to state the earth was at least 1.46 billion years old. The assertion was based on the uranium-lead dating of minerals taken from the Black Hills of South Dakota. From that time on, the location of the world's oldest rock jumped from continent to continent, residing for short periods in the U.S.S.R., South Africa and the Congo. I was delighted to discover that for a short period in the 1960s the world's oldest stone was a 3.1-billion-year-old zircon found in the Beartooth Mountains of Montana. It was coming to know these mountains that eventually led me to write this book.

Notice how helpful it is to sight an occasional person amid these primordial forces: the writer himself, the geologist Arthur Holmes revealing to his presumably stunned colleagues in 1931 that the earth was at least 1.46 billion years old, and the unnamed geologist who only thirty years later jumped that figure to 3.1 billion. We're being allowed to kibitz at the scientists' game of earth-dating—one that's still not over:

Today the world's oldest known rocks are in a formation of twisted gray metamorphic structure on the western coast of Greenland. Dated by the rubidium-strontium method, these rocks are almost 3.8 billion years old. Since some of the rocks are clearly sedimentary in origin, this finding also indicates that the earth had oceans (or at least large bodies of water) on its surface 3.8 billion years ago.

But that still doesn't answer the main question, Trefil says. The question is: How can we go beyond the age of the oldest known rocks to the age of the earth itself?

Radiometric dating cannot be used to determine the age of anything that happened before the melting and differentiation of the earth. In effect, the melting reset all the geological clocks on earth. If we want to go beyond that event to the formation of the earth itself, we will have to use an indirect method of arriving at an estimate.

One such estimate is based on the radiometric dating of meteorites. Both uranium-lead and rubidium-strontium measurements indicate that meteorites striking the earth were formed 4.6 billion years ago. If we believe that these meteorites represent material left over from the construction of the planets, then we say that the earth must have formed at the same time they did—4.6 billion years ago.

A second line of inference is to look at the dating of rocks taken from the moon. Again, we find that standard techniques (primarily potassium-argon) give an age for moon rocks of about 4.6 billion years. The moon, as we know, underwent differentiation only at the surface, and solidified quickly. Consequently, geological clocks on its surface were reset much earlier than those on the earth, and their age is a much better indication of the time of the moon's formation than are the corresponding ages for earth rocks. If you think the earth and the moon formed at the same time, you would conclude that the earth is 4.6 billion years old.

Enough! I have a hard enough time handling three score years and ten. Still, Professor Trefil has warmed up his narrative more than I would have thought possible. He hasn't simply told me the story of the age of the earth; he has told me the even more amazing story of the leap in man's ability to calculate that age—an intellectual feat that takes us from Bishop Ussher's seventeenth-century Biblical surmise (not quite 6,000 years) to the potassium-argon dating of rocks that man has actually gone to the moon to get (4.6 billion years).

This is the human need that writing-across-the-curriculum programs will have to bear in mind in disciplines that take students far beyond the human frame of reference. We want the study of the earth, for instance, to make some connection with the time we spend inhabiting it: How should we think about it? How should we take care of it? Writers and learners will write better and learn more if they understand the "why" of what they are studying.

I put this problem to a group of professors at Boise State University several years ago; we were discussing how to bring writing into the science curriculum. One of them, Monte D. Wilson, professor of geology, said that he tries to expose his students to writing that is excellent both as science and as prose. I asked him if I could see some examples, and he gave me four that amply proved his point. They represented the best of both writing worlds.

The first was every inch a scientific document, complete with tables and topographic maps and published by the United States Government (Geological Survey Professional Paper 596). Entitled "The Catastrophic Late Pleistocene Bonneville Flood in the Snake River Plain, Idaho," it was an exhaustive account by Harold E. Malde of the fieldwork that enabled him to retrace what happened when "Lake Bonneville, at one time in its early history, spilled northward at Red Rock Pass near Preston, Idaho, and suddenly released an enormous volume of water onto the Snake River Plain, leaving a vivid record of its cataclysmic passage."

"Hal Malde's paper is an example of excellent professional writing," Professor Wilson told me. "Although it was intended for professional geologists, it's easily understood by non-scientists. Its scientific content is first-rate; in fact, it won the Geological Society of America's award in 1970 for its contribution to the study of landforms—what we call geomorphology. His style gives you that feeling of interest that's associated with a good story rather than the leaden feeling that's all too often associated with a scientific treatise." Reading it, I could only agree; although the Pleistocene Age was hardly yesterday, in Malde's writing it almost seemed that way:

> Boulders of sedimentary material are especially evident in the railroad pit at Mile 109 and at the upper end of the Grandview Basin, where floodwater was impounded in deep temporary lakes. The basalt boulders are typically very well rounded and obviously have been thoroughly rolled, tumbled and abraded during their passage downstream. . . .

The three other pieces were of a different order. "They're not examples of scientific writing intended for scientists; they're prose writings on scientific topics," Professor Wilson explained. "The earthquake piece by John Muir, for instance, conveys his characteristic reverence for nature, but it also does a nice job of relating earthquakes to landscapes." In fact, I can't imagine a nicer job. This is how the great naturalist recalled the Inyo Earthquake, which struck Yosemite Valley on the night of March 26, 1872. Muir at the time was caretaker of Black's Hotel, under Sentinel Rock.

> In Yosemite Valley, one morning about two o'clock, I was aroused by an earthquake; and though I had never before enjoyed a storm of this sort, the strange, wild thrilling motion and rumbling could not be mistaken, and I ran out of my cabin, both glad and frightened, shouting, "A noble earthquake!" feeling sure I was going to learn something. The shocks were so violent and varied, and succeeded one another so closely, one had to balance in walking as if on the deck of a ship among the waves, and it seemed impossible the high cliffs should escape being shattered. In particular, I feared that the sheer-fronted Sentinel Rock, which rises to a height of

three thousand feet, would be shaken down, and I took shelter back of a big pine, hoping I might be protected from out-bounding boulders, should any come so far. I was now convinced that an earthquake had been the maker of the taluses [in the park], and proof positive came soon enough.

A talus is a pile of rock debris at the foot of a cliff. It's the only geological term Muir had to use; otherwise his language has the dramatic flair of a Victorian novel. Read on:

It was a calm moonlight night, and no sound was heard for the first minute or two save a low muffled underground rumbling and a slight rustling of the agitated trees, as if, in wrestling with the mountains, Nature were holding her breath. Then, suddenly, out of the strange silence and strange motion there came a tremendous roar. The Eagle Rock, a short distance up the valley, had given way, and I saw it falling in thousands of the great boulders I had been studying for so long, pouring to the valley floor in a free curve luminous from friction, making a terribly sublime and beautiful spectacle—an arc of fire fifteen hundred feet across, as true in form and as steady as a rainbow, in the midst of the stupendous roaring rock-storm. The sound was inconceivably deep and broad and earnest, as if the whole earth, like a living creature, had at last found a voice and were calling to her sister planets. It seemed to me that if all the thunder I ever heard were condensed into one roar it would not equal this rock roar at the birth of a mountain talus. Think, then, of the roar that arose to heaven when all the thousands of ancient canyon taluses throughout the length and breadth of the range were simultaneously given birth.

Paragraphs don't come much richer than that. The grandeur of the moment is vividly caught, yet the words are precise and relatively simple.

The main storm was soon over, and, eager to see the new-born talus, I ran up the valley in the moonlight and climbed it before the huge blocks, after their wild fiery flight, had come to complete rest. They were slowly settling into their places, chafing, grating against one another, groaning, and whispering; but no motion was visible except in a stream of small fragments pattering down the face of the cliff at the head of the talus. A cloud of dust particles, the smallest of the boulders, floated out across the whole breadth of the valley and formed a ceiling that lasted until after sunrise; and the air was loaded with the odor of crushed Douglas Spruces, from a grove that had been mowed down and mashed like weeds.

Sauntering about to see what other changes had been made, I found the Indians in the middle of the valley, terribly frightened, of course, fearing that the angry spirits of the rocks were trying to kill them. The few whites wintering in the valley were assembled in front of the old Hutchings Hotel, comparing notes and meditating flight to steadier ground, seemingly as sorely frightened as the Indians. It is always interesting to see people in dead earnest, from whatever cause, and earthquakes make everybody earnest. . . .

Jump forward three quarters of a century to Alan Paton's *Cry, the Beloved Country*. I remember the impact that the novel made when it was published in 1948. It was the first voice to tell us of the pain of South Africa, and as a voice it was not quite like any other in its cadences and its plain strength. I knew all along that it was literature; that's what gave it its grip on the emotions of readers all over the world. But I didn't know that it was also good geology. "Although *Cry, the Beloved Country* was written almost forty years ago," Professor Wilson told me, "it's strikingly relevant today. The short first chapter is a beautifully written description of the importance of ecological principles to social systems."

Here's the first chapter in its entirety:

There is a lovely road that runs from Ixopo into the hills. These hills are grass-covered and rolling, and they are lovely beyond any singing of it. The road climbs seven miles into them, to Carisbrooke; and from there, if there is no mist, you look down on one of the fairest valleys of Africa. About you there is grass and bracken and you may hear the forlorn crying of the titihoya, one of the birds of the veld. Below you is the valley of the Umzimkulu, on its journey from the Drakensberg to the sea; and beyond and behind the river, great hill after great hill; and beyond and behind them, the mountains of Ingeli and East Griqualand.

The grass is rich and matted, you cannot see the soil. It holds the rain and the mist, and they seep into the ground, feeding the streams in every kloof. It is well-tended, and not too many cattle feed upon it; not too many fires burn it, laying bare the soil. Stand unshod upon it, for the ground is holy, being even as it came from the Creator. Keep it, guard it, care for it, for it keeps men, guards men, cares for men. Destroy it and man is destroyed.

Where you stand the grass is rich and matted, you cannot see the soil. But the rich green hills break down. They fall to the valley below, and falling, change their nature. For they grow red and bare; they cannot hold the rain and mist, and the streams are dry in the kloofs. Too many cattle feed upon the grass, and too many fires have burned it. Stand shod upon it, for it is coarse and sharp, and the stones cut under the feet. It is not kept, or guarded, or cared for, it no longer keeps men, guards men, cares for men. The titihoya does not cry here any more.

The great red hills stand desolate, and the earth has torn away like flesh. The lightning flashes over them, the clouds pour down upon them, the dead streams come to life, full of the red blood of the earth. Down in the valleys women scratch the soil that is left, and the maize hardly reaches the height of a man. They are valleys of old men and old women, of mothers and children. The men are away, the young men and the girls are away. The soil cannot keep them any more.

The fourth example was a passage from *A Sand County Almanac,* by the conservationist Aldo Leopold, a book that has many fans, judging by how many people have commended it to me. (For my taste it's a little florid.) Professor Wilson told me that he often finds in Leopold's book a helpful explanation of some phenomenon that his geology class is wrestling with. About the following passage, called "Cheat Takes Over," he said, "My students who are out on field projects often complain about the prickly cheat grass. I ask them to read Leopold's essay in the hope that they'll contemplate the ecological relationships and principles that are so well expressed in it."

As a fourth-generation Manhattanite, my roots deep in the cement, I had never felt the rough hand of cheat grass or even heard of it. Aldo Leopold made me realize that city dwellers are lucky not to have been visited by some of these "uninvited ecological guests."

Ecological stowaways began to arrive with the earliest settlements. The Swedish botanist, Peter Kalm, found most of the European weeds established in New Jersey and New York as early as 1750. They spread as rapidly as the settler's plow could prepare a suitable seedbed.

Others arrived later, from the West, and found thousands of square miles of ready-made seedbed prepared by the trampling hoofs of range livestock. In such cases the spread was often so rapid as to escape recording; one simply woke up one fine spring to find the range dominated by a new weed. A notable instance was the invasion of the intermountain and northwestern foothills by downy chess or cheat grass *(Bromus tectorum)*.

Lest you gain too optimistic an impression of this new ingredient of the melting pot, let me say that cheat is not a grass in the sense of forming a live sod. It is an annual weed of the grass family, like foxtail or crabgrass, dying each fall and reseeding that fall or the next spring. In Europe its habitat is the decaying straw of thatched roofs. The Latin word for roof is *tectum*, hence the label "Brome of the roofs." A plant that can make a living on the roof of a house can also thrive on this rich but arid roof of the continent.

Today the honey-colored hills that flank the northwestern mountains derive their hue not from the rich and useful bunchgrass and wheatgrass which once covered them, but from the inferior cheat which has replaced these native grasses. The motorist who exclaims about the flowing contours that lead his eye upward to far summits is unaware of this substitution. It does not occur to him that hills, too, cover ruined complexions with ecological face powder.

The cause of the substitution is overgrazing. When the too-great herds and flocks chewed and trampled the hide off the foothills, something had to cover the raw eroding earth. Cheat did. . . .

John Muir and Aldo Leopold were among the earliest writers to alert their fellow citizens to the fact that the earth was being mistreated, thereby helping to launch the environmental movement that made "ecology" a household word in the 1960s. In fact, Muir was one of the founders of the Sierra Club. Today, such is the public awareness of the chemical agents polluting our earth, air and water that most of us routinely read geological writing that we would have shied away from a generation ago. There's a newspaper in Colorado that I admire, for instance, called *High Country News*—"A Paper for People Who

Care About the West"—which is devoted solely to environmental matters. Many of its articles deal with the legal and political conflicts between private and public interests that are the daily battleground of conservation. But just as many deal accessibly with subjects that fall within such formal disciplines as geology (mud slides), engineering (flood control) and meteorology (acid rain). The following article, by Ed Marston and Mary Moran, is a typically clear explanation of a geological calamity that befell the area near Redstone in the spring of 1986:

Over the past month, western Colorado's Muddy Creek earthslide has moved an estimated 140 million cubic yards of rock, sand and soil more than 200 feet downslope. This world-class slide, many times greater than Utah's Thistle Slide, which drowned a town, railroad and highway in 1984, has wreaked havoc on a sparsely settled mountain hillside.

Its major effect on man's work has been to close State Highway 133 between the Crystal River Valley and the North Fork Valley. Luckily, very few people live near the slide. But the few residents of this remote high country have suffered. . . .

Although the slide consists of three lobes, one almost a mile wide and extending two miles up the mountain, the lobes aren't moving as solid units. On the average, the 140 million cubic yards of rock, sand and soil are moving together. But each of the lobes has its own internal stresses and strains. Fissures open here, swallowing a stream perhaps or splitting a tree in half. Elsewhere, the ground heaves and humps.

An older state highway, which crosses the slide, presents the most graphic illustration of its effects. As you drive toward the slide from Carbondale the road abruptly ends in a crack, with pasture beyond. It is not until you get out of the car that you can see the rest of the road—a fair distance down the hill. . . .

What has caused this havoc? According to Colorado's state

geologist, John Rold, the slide probably first moved 5,000 to 8,000 years ago. At that time the earth was coming out of its last ice age, and there was abundant water in the soils and flowing above ground. Many Colorado landslides date from this unstable period.

The slide's reactivation this year wasn't a surprise, Rold says. Precipitation has been above average for five years now in western Colorado, building up moisture content in the soils. . . .

Obviously—from these various passages—the earth is not as solid a place as I thought it was. But at least it's visible; if it quakes or slides we can see it shift and try to get out of the way. Not so the sea. That's a world so impenetrable that we can only go there through the mind of a photographer or a filmmaker, who gives us brief glimpses through the gloom, or through a writer, who uses language and scholarship to surmise what life is like on the ocean floor.

No book that I know is more eloquent about these sunken mysteries than Rachel Carson's *The Sea Around Us.* Miss Carson is better known for her later classic, *Silent Spring,* which, by calling attention to the insidious damage that well-meant chemicals like DDT were foisting on the planet, gave the young environmental movement its biggest push in the 1960s. But in *The Sea Around Us* a stylist of vigor and beauty was already at work. Miss Carson was not a writer who chose the sea as her subject; she was an aquatic biologist who could write. In the following passage she brings off two feats—one scientific, the other historical. First she imagines for us a world of creatures in "the sunless sea" that is beyond our own imagining. Then she tells us the story of how scientists began to look for—and finally to receive—scraps of extraordinary information from the deep. Her story has the appeal of every story about scientists stepping into unknown territory and building on the knowledge of their predecessors. But this time the frontier is straight down:

Between the sunlit surface waters of the open sea and the hidden hills and valleys of the ocean floor lies the least known region of the sea. These deep, dark waters, with all their mysteries and their unsolved problems, cover a very considerable part of the earth. The whole world ocean extends over about three fourths of the surface of the globe. If we subtract the shallow areas of the continental shelves and the scattered banks and shoals, where at least the pale ghost of sunlight moves over the underlying bottom, there still remains about half the earth that is covered by miles-deep, lightless water, that has been dark since the world began.

This region has held its secrets more obstinately than any other. Man, with all his ingenuity, has been able to venture only to its threshold. Wearing a diving helmet, he can walk on the ocean floor about 10 fathoms down. He can descend to an extreme limit of about 500 feet in a complete diving suit, so heavily armored that movement is almost impossible, carrying with him a constant supply of oxygen. Only two men in all the history of the world have had the experience of descending, alive, beyond the range of visible light. These men were William Beebe and Otis Barton. In the bathysphere, they reached a depth of 3028 feet in the open ocean off Bermuda, in the year 1934. Barton alone, in a steel sphere known as the benthoscope, descended to the great depth of 4500 feet off California, in the summer of 1949.

Although only a fortunate few can ever visit the deep sea, the precise instruments of the oceanographer, recording light penetration, pressure, salinity and temperature, have given us the materials with which to reconstruct in imagination these eerie, forbidding regions. Unlike the surface waters, which are sensitive to every gust of wind, which know day and night, respond to the pull of sun and moon, and change as the seasons change, the deep waters are a place where change comes slowly, if at all. Down beyond the reach of the sun's rays there is no alternation of light and darkness. There is rather an unending night, as old as the sea itself. For most of its creatures, groping their way endlessly through its black waters, it must be a place of hunger, where food is scarce and hard to find, a shelterless place where there is no sanctuary from ever-present enemies, where one can only move on and on, from birth to death, through an endless night, confined as in a prison to his own particular layer of the sea.

They used to say that nothing could live in the deep sea. It was a belief that must have been easy to accept, for without proof to the contrary, how could anyone conceive of life in such a place?

A century ago the British biologist Edward Forbes wrote: "As we descend deeper and deeper into this region, the inhabitants become more and more modified, and fewer and fewer, indicating our approach to an abyss where life is either extinguished, or exhibits but a few sparks of its lingering presence." Yet Forbes urged further exploration of "this vast deep-sea region" to settle forever the question of the existence of life at great depths.

Even then the evidence was accumulating. Sir John Ross, during his exploration of the arctic seas in 1818, had brought up from a depth of 1000 fathoms mud in which there were worms, "thus proving there was animal life in the bed of the ocean notwithstanding the darkness, stillness, silence and immense pressure produced by more than a mile of superincumbent water."

Then from the surveying ship *Bulldog*, examining a proposed northern route for a cable from Faroe to Labrador in 1860, came another report. The *Bulldog*'s sounding line, which at one place had been allowed to lie for some time on the bottom at a depth of 1260 fathoms, came up with thirteen starfish clinging to it. Through these starfish, the ship's naturalist wrote, "the deep has sent forth the long coveted message." But not all the zoologists of the day were prepared to accept the message. Some doubters asserted that the starfish had "convulsively embraced" the line somewhere on the way back to the surface.

By quoting the ship's naturalist and his wonderful phrase about the long coveted message, Miss Carson keeps herself in the story, notifying us that her interest is more than scientific. As a historian she has obviously buried herself in the logs and journals of the men who sailed on the *Bulldog,* looking for the human element that every writer needs to bring a scientific achievement to life. She also gives us a strong sense of elapsing time, reminding us of the sequential nature of scientific progress. The next two paragraphs have the cumulative thrill of discovery:

In the same year, 1860, a cable in the Mediterranean was raised for repairs from a depth of 1200 fathoms. It was found to be heavily encrusted with corals and other sessile animals that had attached themselves at an early stage of development and grown to maturity over a period of months or years. There was not the slightest chance that they had become entangled in the cable as it was being raised to the surface.

Then the *Challenger* set out from Portsmouth in the year 1872 and traced a course around the globe. From bottoms lying under miles of water, from silent deeps carpeted with red clay ooze, and from all the lightless intermediate depths, net-haul after net-haul of strange and fantastic creatures came up and were spilled out on the decks. Poring over the weird beings thus brought up for the first time into the light of day, beings no man had ever seen before, the *Challenger* scientists realized that life existed even on the deepest floor of the abyss.

The ultimate frontier, of course, is what I'll call the sky, using that simple word to hold at bay the terrors of infinite space. It's no fun to think about infinity and no cinch to write about it. Again, it helps to look for some human link, and, again, I'll take an example from *Meditations at 10,000 Feet,* by James Trefil, who, when last heard from in this chapter, had given us the hardly comforting news that the earth is 4.6 billion years old. Here he describes how an American astronomer earlier in this century discovered that the Milky Way was only a fragment of a much larger story.

The best place to start is to recall why it is that telescopes are located on mountaintops. The purpose of a telescope is to gather light that has been emitted by distant sources. By analyzing this light we learn about the emitting object, whether that object is a nearby ship, a neighboring planet or a galaxy at the edge of the observable universe. Sometimes this knowledge is rather straightforward—we learn the size and shape of the thing being studied, more or less as we would by looking at it with our naked eye. In other cases we subject the incoming light to a more sophisticated analysis and determine facts about the objects such as temperature and chemical composition. But no matter what type of analysis we do, we are limited by the amount of light available to our instrument.

We normally think of the earth's atmosphere as being completely transparent, for we can often see things a surprising distance away. . . . From such everyday experiences we conclude that light can easily be transmitted through a thickness of atmosphere ranging up to 100 miles. We also know that the earth's atmosphere forms a fairly thin layer around our planet. "Outer space" is generally reckoned to start at an altitude around 50,000 feet—roughly ten miles. This means that light entering the atmosphere has to travel at most ten miles to get to the surface. Why, then, do we go to the trouble of building roads to the tops of mountains to put our telescopes a few miles closer to the source of light? Wouldn't a telescope function just as well at sea level?

The answer depends on what we want to study. If we want to look at a relatively bright, nearby object, sea-level telescopes will work perfectly well. Galileo saw spots on the sun and mountains on the moon from his balcony in Florence, and the planets Neptune and Uranus were discovered by telescopes located on the ground near major European cities (Berlin and London). Even today the study of the positions of nearby stars (a field known as astrometry) is carried out with such telescopes, one of which is in downtown Pittsburgh. The accurate determination of the position of nearby stars has great practical importance, since it is by sightings of such stars that satellites are navigated. Nevertheless such studies do not occupy the main attention of professional astronomers.

A much more likely target for a telescope being used in frontier research is a distant faint object, be it star, galaxy or interstellar cloud. Since the mid-nineteenth century, astronomers have not been content with finding out where objects are in the sky; they have moved on to asking what the objects are. Answering this sort of question requires a sophisticated analysis of incoming light. . . .

Such sophistication can't be achieved at ground level, Trefil points out, because of "light pollution" from cities, because of the greater density and distortion of the atmosphere at lower altitudes, and because "if an object is very distant from the earth it is likely to appear quite small, regardless of its true size," its light almost too faint to be analyzed. Hence the flight to the mountaintops.

The beginning of twentieth-century astronomy can be traced to the installation of a 100-inch telescope on top of Mount Wilson near Los Angeles in the early 1920s. Edwin Hubble, using the unprecedented resolving power of his new instrument, was able to establish that our Milky Way was only one of a large number of galaxies in the universe. The technique he used was simple, at least in principle.

A certain class of stars known as Cepheid variables grow alternately bright and dim over periods of weeks or months. By examining such stars in the neighborhood of the earth, it had been established that the time it took each star to go through one of its cycles depended on how much total light it emitted. This means that if you measure the amount from the variable star light that falls on a telescope you can tell how far away it is. If the star appears faint while its period indicates that it is actually very bright, you conclude that it must be far away. Similarly, if it appears bright but its period indicates that it must be faint, it must be close by.

Because Hubble could actually pick out individual stars in the Andromeda Nebula he was able to establish that its distance from the earth was over 200 million light-years. Contrasting this 200 million to the greatest distance between stars in the Milky Way—a "mere" 100,000 light-years—Hubble argued that the collection of stars in the Andromeda Nebula constituted an "island universe" like our own. Overnight, the horizons of astronomy expanded from the study of a single galaxy to the study of the collection of billions of galaxies that make up our universe.

Hubble's discovery, with its immense implications for the place of mankind in the universe, depended on his ability to make out a single star in a galaxy hundreds of millions of light-years away. This is a familiar pattern in the history of science; the greatest intellectual advances often depend on our ability to deal with the grubby details of instrumentation.

7.   Art and Artists

I'm often surprised by the art I see in the homes of highly literate people. The books so carefully arrayed on their bookshelves reveal them to be men and women of knowledge and taste. But the painters hanging on their walls are the equivalent of writers they wouldn't be caught dead reading—Danielle Steel, say, or Kahlil Gibran. Obviously visual literacy isn't as important to them as verbal literacy. Or maybe they think that because art is all around them they don't need to make an effort to learn about it—the kind of effort they made with all those books. But art is a language that has to be studied like any other language.

I don't mean to suggest that a visitor entering my apartment will think he has stumbled into the National Gallery by mistake. If the art on its walls and its shelves is more than ordinarily interesting it's because my wife has done her best to educate me and because we have looked at art for many years in many parts of the world. Still, I feel that I'm only slightly more visually literate than the next man. Whenever I listen to an artist or an art historian I'm struck by how much they *see* and how much they *know*—and how much I don't.

Good art writing should therefore do at least two things. It should teach us how to look: at art, architecture, sculpture, photography and all the other visual components of our daily landscape. And it should give us the information we need to understand what we're looking at.

One teacher who had this capacity was George Nelson, the American designer whose many gifts to urban man include the pedestrian mall—the city street that's closed to cars. Nelson spent much of his fifty-year career with the Herman Miller company, designing the innovative office products that gave the firm much of its renown. I met him once, briefly, in the mid-1960s, when I was assigned to write a magazine article about a bold new system of office furniture he had created. I had never heard of him and knew nothing of the reverence in which he was held by the design world, but I have never forgotten the playfulness of his mind. I also remember how important he felt good writing was. After that, right up to his death in 1986, whenever I saw one of his articles I realized that part of his enormous influence came from his ability to present visual ideas with clarity, humanity and humor.

Here's a passage from his lively book *How to See:*

Visual decoding takes place at a great variety of levels, and in this sense it is not basically different from the use of any language. When the Lone Ranger and his faithful Tonto stop at some scuff marks in the desert and conclude that a band of outlaws has passed that way, carrying a ravishing blond captive on a strawberry roan, and that the leader's horse had recently thrown a shoe, we marvel at their skill in getting so much information out of some disturbed earth. What these two would do if confronted by Picasso's *Guernica* is another question. Reading a painting takes another set of skills. . . .

In visual reading, like verbal reading, the completeness of the reading relates directly to the quality of the reader's stored information. A cat may look at a king, as the old saying goes, but the visual message is more interesting if the onlooker also knows what a king is. Visual communication, therefore, is not unlike other kinds of communication in that it is broadcast and received and in that it uses a code of language which has to be intelligible to the receiver.

This becomes instantly apparent when we turn to modern painting. In the art of the nineteenth century and earlier, a painting was invariably a picture of something. You could look at it and see that the subject was a dog or a family group, a still life, a landscape. At the popular level of viewing, identifying the subject and perhaps the sentiment was sufficient. In this sense traditional painting is not unlike what we get on a TV screen: a story illustrated by photographic images. If the police are chasing the villain, we see cars screaming around curves, going off cliffs; gunplay; and the inevitable finale. . . .

It is when subject matter, perspective and other familiar elements in painting disappear, as in modern painting, that the absence of nonverbal comprehension comes out into the open. Why does a museum show a cluster of four aluminum boxes as art? What gives value of any kind to a painting which is nothing more than a white or black surface? Léger's people look like boilers: where has he seen such people? Why do the Cubists chop up guitars, tables, newspapers and bottles and put them back together all wrong? The usual responses, going back at least sixty years to the New York Armory Show, are that the artists are crazy; it is fairly standard for people to react to newness with nervous hostility. It is also possible, however, that the artists are sane and that the world they are painting is crazy.

This is enjoyable stuff, lighthearted in tone but serious in its ideas. I especially like the sentence about the cat looking at a king. Like a well-constructed joke, it makes its point at the end and thereby takes us by surprise—always a tonic in writing. It reminds me of a sentence in *Walden,* by that underestimated humorist Henry David Thoreau: "The cart before the horse is neither beautiful nor useful." Thoreau was complaining about people who don't present their facts in logical order. Nelson was saying that nobody can understand art unless he brings to it certain necessary information.

Also notice how Nelson anchors his writing in specific detail. He doesn't talk about "Cubism"; he talks about "the Cubists"— real people—and how they broke various conventions to create the ism. He makes us *see* paintings by Picasso and Braque and Léger; if we don't know the actual paintings, we still get the point of what the Cubists did. We have been given a picture.

Today the most consistently graceful writer about art, at least for my money—the cost of buying the daily and Sunday *New York Times*—is that paper's art critic John Russell. A broadly educated man, he wears his erudition lightly. I never think of him as a scholar assaulting me with how much he knows, but as a teacher eager to share a lifelong passion for his subject. The following passage is the introduction to his book *Meanings of Modern Art*. It starts with deceptive simplicity—in fact, with sixteen consecutive one-syllable words, perhaps the world record for an art historian. But before it's over we have been taken on a trip of remarkable range and subtlety.

When art is made new, we are made new with it. We have a sense of solidarity with our own time, and of psychic energies shared and redoubled, which is just about the most satisfying thing that life has to offer. "If that is possible," we say to ourselves, "then everything is possible"; a new phase in the history of human awareness has been opened up, just as it was opened up when people first read Dante, or first heard Bach's 48 preludes and fugues, or first learned from *Hamlet* and *King Lear* that the complexities and contradictions of human nature could be spelled out on the stage.

This being so, it is a great exasperation to come face to face with new art and not make anything of it. Stared down by something that we don't like, don't understand and can't believe in, we feel personally affronted, as if our identity as reasonably alert and responsive human beings had been called into question. We ought to be having a good time, and we aren't. More than that, an important part of life is being withheld from us; for if any one thing is certain in this world it is that art is there to help us live, and for no other reason.

Note how quickly Russell establishes rapport with his readers. He knows how stupid we feel in the presence of art we can't fathom, how terrible we feel to be left out. Feeling left out is one of the oldest and worst ways of feeling terrible, as every child knows who remains unchosen after the rite of "choosing up sides" or who is sent to play right field, that Siberia of childhood baseball, where (with luck) no ball will be hit. Russell assures us that we're not jerks. Trust me, he says, I'm one of you. Of course he's not—he's much brighter, and we want him to be. But we're also glad he knows how it feels to be one of us.

Continuing, Russell writes that "for hundreds of years, and on many matters of supreme importance, art had the edge over all other sources."

It gave out the truth about this world and the next one. It encapsulated history. It told us what people wiser than ourselves were thinking. It told the stories that everyone wanted to hear . . . answered the great riddles, filled in the gaps in our general knowledge, and laid Eternity on the line. Above all, it gave reassurance; it told us what we wanted to hear—that experience was not formless and illegible, that man could speak to man without the obstructions of language.

Art restored to us the lost wholeness, the sensation of being at one with Nature, and at one with society, which we crave from the moment of birth. . . . So we are quite right to be dismayed when art seems to shift its ground in ways that we find difficult to follow. Still less do we like to think that art might one day peter out. We should prefer to think—and in my opinion we are quite right to think—that the masterpieces of our own day can perfectly well stand comparison with the great achievements of the past.

But the anxiety remains, Russell writes, because art has gradually altered its purpose and recoded its messages.

It was in the second half of the nineteenth century that art was relieved of certain of the duties which it had been carrying out on society's behalf and became free to look into its own nature. The duties in question had been many and varied. Philip IV of Spain never doubted that when his troops won a famous victory his court painter Velásquez was the best man to commemorate it. When Marat was murdered in his bath in 1793, it was by popular demand, almost, that Jacques-Louis David made haste to paint *Marat Assassinated*. When the Houses of Parliament burned down in 1834, art gave us our most memorable account of what happened: J.M.W. Turner was on hand to tell how the great scarf of flame unwound itself high in the night sky. Art had no rival on such occasions. It gave us what we could get nowhere else. Nor was the artist simply a passive recorder: when the French frigate *Méduse* was lost in particularly ghastly circumstances in 1816, it was a painter, Théodore Géricault, who brought the matter out of the newspapers and onto a deeper level of concern.

In paintings such as the ones I have named, people were told what they wanted to know, and told it in a way that allied power to concision and eloquence to understanding. . . . That is to say that we have a deeper understanding of old age and are the readier to meet it ourselves if we have studied Joseph Wright of Derby's *The Old Man and Death*. We have a deeper understanding of what it means for one person to give himself to another if we have studied Rembrandt's *The Jewish Bride*. We have a deeper understanding of what it means to love the world and lose it if we have studied the valedictory images of the dying Watteau. Marcel Proust was one of the most observant men who ever lived, but he spoke for all of us when he wrote, "Until I saw Chardin's paintings I never realized how much beauty lay around me in my parents' house, in the half-cleared table, in the corner of a tablecloth left awry, in the knife beside the empty oyster-shell."

But as the nineteenth century came to an end, Russell writes, people began to have needs that the Old Masters couldn't satisfy because those needs didn't exist when the Old Masters were around. New masters were needed to speak to the unprecedented despairs and horrors that the twentieth century would bring:

Poussin in his *Massacre of the Innocents* gave us an unforgettable image of a human mouth wide open in a scream; but because he was a great classical artist that scream was incidental to his Olympian overview of the scene as a whole. It fell to Edvard Munch, in 1893, to give us an image of a shriek which (in Munch's own words) "pierced the whole of nature" and stood for a sudden, vast and quite irresistible sensation of panic and dismay. Europe needed just that picture at just that time, and nothing from the past could have taken its place. In 1945, when the complete facts about the Nazi concentration camps were available for the first time, Europe needed Picasso's *The Charnel House*, which was the more powerful for its sobriety of color, its condensed, pressed-down, claustrophobic imagery and its refusal to itemize what was so readily to hand in print. The best art of the past hundred years came into being on occasions when nothing from the past would fill the bill.

As a journalist Russell is no less mindful that art and life are connected. Several years ago he went to Flagstaff, Arizona, to see what he called "the most ambitious work of art now under construction in the United States"—the reshaping of Roden Crater, the crater of an extinct volcano, by the artist James Turrell. This is how he began his report in the *Times:*

> One of the undecided problems of our time is the final status of the earthwork as artwork—the huge construction that is set up in remote places, often at great expense, and is necessarily available to only a very few people. Is it a moral breakthrough, a parable of purity that could be acted out in no other way, and a lasting enrichment of human awareness? Or is it the very rich man's last ridiculous toy and the natural descendant of the eighteenth-century folly that looked like a castle, a bridge or a tower and served no practical purpose at all?

The query, so refreshingly put, sends us in many directions, for, as Russell goes on to explain, Turrell's purpose at Roden Crater is "to put the visitor into a direct relationship with our universe that can be obtained in no other way and in no other place. His calculations will take care of the visitor who will come to the crater thousands of years from now. They will take care of an alignment of the moon that will occur once every 18.6 years."

Not waiting for the artist's work to be finished—some time in the 1990s—Russell lay down in the bottom of the crater and opened his eyes wide. "What happens then," he writes, "is that we experience the universe as a perfect sphere, with the rim of the crater—more than 5,000 feet in diameter—as its terrestrial frontier. All that is contingent or superfluous is abolished. As far as is possible on earth, movements and noise do not exist."

Think how many disciplines that one article starts us musing about: astronomy and geology, ecology and aesthetics, physics and psychology, philosophy and religion. It originated, however, as an article about art; someone had to write about one artist's vision before we could begin to muse. Writing is often our only avenue into a special world. Not everybody has a talent for painting, or for the piano, or for dance. But we can write our way into the artist's head and into his problems and solutions. Or we can go there with another writer, as, in this case, we have been taken by John Russell into the mind of James Turrell. The literature is all around us, available as a model to every writer or student who is trying to make complex ideas clear.

Perspective, for instance, is a complex idea, surely not reducible to words. But consider this passage from *Prints & People*, by A. Hyatt Mayor, who was curator of prints at the Metropolitan Museum of Art for more than forty years. I first noticed his handiwork when I attended an exhibition of prints at the Met and found that the accompanying labels were a pleasure to read—something I hadn't thought possible. I had always thought museum labels were meant as some kind of penance for the museumgoer. Why else were they written with such solemnity, printed in white type on a beige mat and hung at a height ideal for a child of nine?

Hyatt Mayor's labels not only told me what I needed to know; they were written with grace and humor and were unfailingly human, never forgetting that the artists who made the prints—and the people depicted in the prints—were as important as the technical process that produced them. Above all, the labels conveyed tremendous enjoyment. This was the writing of a man in love with prints.

When *Prints & People* was published in 1972, near the end of Mayor's career, it captured in a book all the qualities I had savored on the Met's walls. I've chosen the following passage because it explains a technical subject—perspective—in chronological order, in personal detail and with clarity.

After the antique world and the Middle Ages had seen objects singly and separately, the Renaissance began to embed things in a continuous matrix of space. Perhaps as early as 1424 some Tuscan painters and mathematicians correlated the artist's sensuous impressions with the scientist's intellectual analysis. Disciplines so distinct could parley in Renaissance Italy, where a man might still aspire to know something about everything. Scientists needed art to clarify the world's complexity, and artists needed scientists to form principles for analyzing appearances. With mathematical perspective a painter could depict objects in their "real" size within an imaginary framework stretching to the horizon. The artifice enabled a Florentine to engrave the first convincing print of a city as only a hawk could then see it.

From 1483 to 1499, perspective was elaborated as an end in itself in Milan by two Tuscans, Leonardo da Vinci and Fra Luca Pacioli, leading to Pacioli's publication of the first series of perspective renderings. These puzzles stimulated Germans to contrive even more outlandish fantasies as perspective grew into a game for astonishment. While Pacioli was still working on his book, the Tuscan discovery somehow reached Jean Pèlerin, a canon of the cathedral of Toul [in France], who used it for the first clear manual of perspective drawing. The French genius for discovering charm at home inspired the most personal and endearing of all perspective illustrations. These are the first prints that present rooms that we might settle into as we explore the canon's wine cellar, his chapter house, his courtyard with an espaliered tree, and even his bedroom. The very coziness of these woodcuts may have kept them from circulating as widely as the formal instructions given to a more pedantic age by the great baroque architect Vignola. This Roman's foreshortening of facades from a mole's-eye point of view completed the lesson of Mantegna by showing baroque painters how to open ceilings upward through an illusion of soaring colonnades into clouds and the toes of lolling gods.

In Mayor's book each of these examples is keyed to an adjacent picture of the woodcut or etching or engraving he has just described. We see the hawk's view of Florence, the octahedron of Pacioli, the three-dimensional whimsies of Hans Lencker, the French canon's cozy bedroom, and Vignola's intricate arrangement of balconies, columns and vaulted ceilings as they might look to a slightly drunken mole. The pictures complement the words, fixing the printmaker's achievement in the reader's eye. But the marvel is how well the words do the job on their own.

Several hundred pages and three centuries later, Mayor is still going like a thoroughbred horse, stepping high and relishing the moment. Notice, below, not only how much information he imparts in one paragraph; also notice the wonder that he brings to the life and the work of the man he is writing about.

The great Chinese ink painters came from a bureaucratic aristocracy trained to semipictorial writing. Although European gentlefolk used to be taught to draw as they were taught to write, the aristocracy of Europe, so rich in remarkable authors, has produced only one remarkable artist: Count Henri-Marie-Raymond de Toulouse-Lautrec Monfa. Lautrec would probably have painted no better than his father if the breaking of both his legs in his teens had not saved him from wasting his life hunting with his cousins. Case-hardened with an aristocrat's contempt for middle-class circumspection, he threw himself into the Paris of prostitutes and hoofers, who also had to put on a show and shrug off suffering with a jest. His fever for living burned out his life when he was thirty-six. He had drawn since he was a baby. After the sketchiest instruction in painting, he found in Degas and in Japanese prints the sifting of appearances that he needed for summing up a person or an

animal in a few tingling lines. This pictorial shorthand looked
like caricature—the distortion of a physical feature—but actually expressed an insight as innocent, and therefore as alarming, as a child's. Looking upward from his child's height, he
caught people at startling angles in pictures to be hung high.
He exercised his command of line and his joy in color through
printers trained in color lithography by Chéret. Lautrec drew
his first color lithograph for a poster when he was twenty-six.
In the ten years that he yet had to live, his oils, vibrant though
they often are, changed the course of art less than his litho-
graphs, and especially his posters, which still startle by their
strategy of attack. When their yellow and orange and black
first flared in the gaslight of the boulevards, no one could miss
the fact that art had taken a new turn.

Take one last look at the style. Seemingly exuberant, it's actually very spare, relying for its panache on individual words
chosen to express a precise meaning: vivid nouns (hoofers, gaslight), working adjectives (tingling lines, startling angles, vibrant oils), strong verbs (burned out, flared). It has no flab;
Mayor says what he wants to say in as many words as he needs
to say it—and no more.

Also notice what a pleasure it is to be in the company of a
writer with enthusiasm for his subject. It doesn't matter what
the subject is; I want an ichthyologist to be as committed to fish
as Mayor is to prints—to make me think there's nothing more
important to him. This is the personal connection that every
reader wants to make with a writer; if we care about the writer
we'll follow him into subjects that we could have sworn we
never wanted to know about. The blind attachment of a hobbyist to his hobby is as interesting a life force as the hobby itself.

Of all the visual arts, none is more compelling than photography. Its directness speaks so powerfully to our everyday experience that we take it for granted, seldom pausing to ask what

made a great photograph great. As every tourist knows who has pointed a camera at the Grand Canyon, the difference between a good photograph and a great one is as wide as the Grand Canyon. What is that difference—what mysterious combination of art, technique, light, eye, personality, patience and luck? Can it be explained?

A book that does this for me is *Looking at Photographs*, by John Szarkowski, curator of the department of photography at the Museum of Modern Art. There may be a better writer about the subject, but I can't imagine who it would be. Selecting one hundred pictures from the museum's collection, Szarkowski has written a brief essay about each one that distills just what we need to know about the photographer, his body of work and the picture being discussed. Here are two excerpts:

> Ansel Adams photographed the [Old Faithful] geyser on at least three separate occasions during the early forties, and produced pictures that are profoundly different from each other. The difference is due not to a willful act of artistic interpretation, but rather to the precision of Adams's sensibility: He saw what was there not in vague and general terms, but with a rigorous exactitude. The problem (as Cézanne put it) was to realize his sensation.
>
> Much of the best photography of the past generation has concerned itself with giving permanent form to the ephemeral. This concern has expressed itself not only in the analysis of that swarming flux of movement within which Cartier-Bresson found his *decisive moment,* but also in the approach to subjects that the casual observer might think static. A landscape does not move in the conventional sense, but it changes constantly in other ways, most notably through the agency of light. Ansel Adams attuned himself more precisely than any photographer before him to a visual understanding of the specific quality of the light that fell on a specific place at a

specific moment. For Adams the natural landscape is not a fixed and solid sculpture but an insubstantial image, as transient as the light that continually redefines it. This sensibility to the specificity of light was the motive that forced Adams to develop his legendary photographic technique. This brilliant technique might be a millstone around the neck of a photographer who did not need it; for Adams nothing less would suffice to describe his subject.

Shifting from the apparent stillness of nature to the perpetual motion of man, Szarkowski gives us a picture of Richard Avedon that is itself like a negative coming into focus as we see the photographer rejecting his earlier vision and deciding that what he wants is its exact opposite:

Even in the early years of his work as a fashion photographer, Richard Avedon was much interested in motion, or rather in the *sense* of motion, since his interest was not analytical but hortatory. As a young photographer in the early fifties Avedon seemed to think that motion was intrinsically a good thing. It is possible that Avedon was in fact one of the architects, unwitting or otherwise, of the Jet Set concept, which was based on the premise that people with style do not alight. Among his many memorable portraits, it is difficult to call one to mind that shows the subject sitting down.

In the beginning Avedon attempted to deal with the subject of motion in a rather literal way, by shooting moving subjects at slow shutter speeds, thus describing forms that tended to resemble feathery-edged projectiles. Some viewers felt that these pictures expressed movement. Whether they did or not, they did not describe a great deal about the object in motion. Perhaps for this reason Avedon later radically revised his approach to the problem. He decided (it would seem) that the most interesting thing that photography could do with movement was destroy it, and show its crystal-clear fossil, suspended in perpetuity, like the once-human figures disinterred at Vesuvius, seemingly overtaken in mid-stride; or, more nearly, like faces illuminated by a catastrophic explosion, the significance of which has not yet registered in their expressions. As the newspapers prove again each day, there is something fascinating and subtly disturbing about a photograph of a person open-mouthed in speech. The effect can be comic or ludicrous or tragic, but the root cause is the same. Life has been arrested.

Along with the vigor of the style and the photographic clarity of its images—the feathery-edged projectiles and the crystal-clear fossil—a quality that I like in Szarkowski's writing is confidence. This is a man with hard-won knowledge of a subject that requires an understanding of both a creative process and a technical process, and he states his opinions boldly; there is nothing feathery-edged about them. A writer who undertakes to be a tour leader can't afford to be bashful. We want a guide who is in command.

Good art writing should above all help us to see, just as good music writing should help us to hear, and its domain can be as wide as the world we live in. Often, in fact, we need to be shown what is right before our eyes. The graphic designer Paul Rand, in his book *A Designer's Art,* notes that although the *Oxford English Dictionary* devotes two columns to "graphics" and four to "design," most people don't know what is meant by "graphic design." The term "commercial art," he says, is probably the one that comes closest to describing his métier, but "snobbery and the lack of clarity about its scope have contributed to its gradual disappearance." Here's his own definition: "A graphic designer is one who creates ideas that are expressed in words and/or pictures and generally solves problems of visual communication. Items that require the work of a graphic designer before they can be printed or produced include price tags, catalogues, newspapers, magazines, posters, brochures, advertisements, books, book jackets, stationery, logos, packaging, product nomenclature (nameplates), signs—in short, anything involving the visual manipulation of words and/or pictures."

Rand's own ventures into most of these forms have so brilliantly solved the particular problem that our eye now accepts his designs as part of the American landscape. But there was nothing haphazard about their birth. The IBM logo, for instance, is one of his most famous creations. I've stared at it for five years on different word processors, never noticing that its three letters pose a severe design problem because of their increasing width—a problem Rand solved, as he explains in *A Designer's Art*, by invoking one of the most historically helpful and pleasing of all visual aids:

> Nature has striped the zebra. Man has striped his flags and awnings, ties and shirts. For the typographer, stripes are rules; for the architect they are a means of creating optical illusions. Stripes are dazzling, sometimes hypnotic, usually happy. They are universal. They have adorned the walls of houses, churches and mosques. Stripes attract attention.
>
> The stripes of the IBM logo serve primarily as an attention-getting device. They take commonplace letters out of the realm of the ordinary. They are memorable. They suggest efficiency and speed. The recent spate of striped logos in the marketplace attests to their effectiveness.
>
> Visually, stripes superimposed on a cluster of letters tend to tie them together. This is especially useful for complex groupings such as the letters IBM, in which each character gets progressively wider, thereby creating a somewhat uncomfortable, open-ended sequence.

Note the astonishing tightness of that passage. In 140 words Rand tells us everything a layman needs to know about the history of stripes in visual design and the application of that history to one of the memorable symbols of our times. Also notice what the style tells us about the man. He's more than a great designer; he's a humanist and a teacher—someone we'd like to have designing for us. The style *is* the man—as it always should be.

One of the most potent elements in our daily landscape, affecting everything we read, is the typeface. Typefaces have always made a big difference to me. The bedroom of my boyhood years was so crammed with the artifacts of two hobbies— printing and baseball—that to reach my bed I had to thread a path between, on one side, a Chandler & Price printing press, a rack of drawers of assorted typefaces and a shelf of books by type designers and, on the other side, an immense hoard of Big League Gum cards, a mountain of back issues of *Baseball* magazine and a stack of books by authors like Babe Ruth. The room smelled faintly of grape, that being the purported flavor of the gum. I studied the typography books as intently as I studied the batting averages on the gum cards, endlessly reading in typefaces of different sizes and fonts the same expedient sentence containing every letter of the alphabet, "The quick brown fox jumped over the lazy sleeping dog," or its far more interesting little brother, "Pack my box with five dozen liquor jugs." From all that looking I developed strong feelings about the subtle gradations that typecutters and printers have achieved in Roman letter forms over the centuries and how those forms can work for or against the emotional intentions of an author.

So subjective a process might seem hard to describe in writing, but many printers and designers have done it. One of them was the British typographer Beatrice Warde:

[My first generalization] is that before any question of physical or literary suitability must come the question of whether the face itself is tolerable or intolerable as a version of the Roman alphabet. If a single letter is warped or snub; if the letters, however pretty in themselves, do not combine automatically into words; if the fourth consecutive page begins to dazzle and irk the eye, and in general if the pages cannot be read with subconscious but very genuine pleasure, that type is intolerable, and that is all there is about it. There are bad types and good types, and the whole science and art of typography begins after the first category has been set aside.

The second generalization is, briefly, that the thing is worth doing. It does genuinely matter that a designer should take trouble and take delight in his choice of typefaces. The trouble and delight are taken not merely "for art's sake" but for the sake of something so subtly and intimately connected with all that is human that it can be described by no other phrase than "the humanities." If "the tone of voice" of a typeface does not count, then nothing counts that distinguishes man from the other animals. The twinkle that softens a rebuke; the martyr's super-logic and the child's intuition; the fact that a fragment of moss can pull back into the memory a whole forest—these are proofs that there is reality in the imponderable, and that not only notation but connotation is part of the proper study of mankind.

The best part of typographic wisdom lies in this study of connotation, the suitability of form to content. People who love ideas must have a love of words, and that means, given a chance, they will take a vivid interest in the clothes which words wear. The more they like to think, the more they will be shocked by any discrepancy between a lucid idea and a murky typesetting. They will become ritualists and dialecticians. They will use such technically indefensible words as "romantic," "chill" and "jaunty" to describe different type-

faces. If they are wise, they will always admit that they are
dealing with processes of the subconscious mind, mere deft
servants of the goddess Literature.

Remember connotation, therefore, if you write about the
visual arts; there's almost always more to looking at art than
meets the eye. Memory and imagination, for instance, are powerfully at work in how we process what we see, as the English
novelist Aldous Huxley points out in *The Art of Seeing*, a book
in which he describes his "visual re-education" from a condition
that had left him almost blind by the age of twenty-five:

> The capacity for perception depends upon the amount, the
> kind and the availability of past experiences. But past experi-
> ences exist for us only in the memory. Therefore it is true to
> say that perception depends upon memory. Closely related to
> memory is imagination, which is the power of recombining
> memories in novel ways, so as to make mental constructions
> different from anything actually experienced in the past.
>
> The extent to which perception and, consequently, vision
> are dependent on memory and imagination is a matter of
> everyday experience. We see familiar things more clearly than
> when we see objects about which we have no stock of memo-
> ries. The old seamstress, who cannot read without glasses, can
> see to thread her needle with the naked eye. Why? Because
> she is more familiar with needles than with print. A man who
> can work all day at the office without undue fatigue of the eyes
> is worn out by an hour at the museum and comes home with
> a splitting headache. Why? Because at the office he is following
> a regular routine and looking at words and figures, the like of
> which he looks at every day; whereas in the museum every-
> thing is strange, novel and outlandish.
>
> Or take the case of the lady who is terrified of snakes and
> who mistakes what to everyone else is obviously a length of

rubber tubing for an enormous viper. Her vision, as tested on the eye chart, is normal. Why, then, does she see what isn't there? Because her imagination had been in the habit of using old memories of snakes to construct alarming images of them, and under the influence of her imagination her mind misinterpreted the *sensa* connected with the rubber tubing in such a way that she vividly "saw" a viper.

I'll give the last word to E. H. Gombrich, the eminent art historian, not only because of his eminence but because one premise of this book is that the sciences and the humanities are more inseparable than we like to think. The following passage, though ostensibly about art, is as good an example of science writing as you'll find in these pages—clear, vivid, elegant and always grounded in details we recognize from our own experience. It's from a book whose title is as provocative as the passage itself—*Art and Illusion: A Study in the Psychology of Pictorial Representation.*

What we get on the retina, whether we are chickens or human beings, is a welter of dancing light points stimulating the sensitive rods and cones that fire their messages into the brain. What we see is a stable world. It takes an effort of the imagination and a fairly complex apparatus to realize the tremendous gulf that exists between the two.

Consider any object, such as a book or a piece of paper. When we scan it with our two eyes it projects upon our two retinas a restless, flitting pattern of light of various wave lengths and intensities. This pattern will hardly ever repeat itself exactly—the angle at which we look, the light, the size of our pupils, all these will have changed. The white light that a piece of paper reflects when turned toward the window is a multiple of what it reflects when turned away. It is not that we do not notice some change; indeed, we must if we want to form an estimate of the illumination.

But we are never conscious of the objective degree of all these changes unless we use what psychologists call a "reduction screen," in essence a peephole that makes us see a speck of color but masks off its relationships. Those who have used this magic instrument report the most striking discoveries. A white handkerchief in the shade may be objectively darker than a lump of coal in the sunshine. We rarely confuse the one with the other because on the whole the lump of coal will be the blackest patch in our field of vision, the handkerchief the whitest, and it is relative brightness that matters and that we are aware of. The coding process begins while en route between the retina and our conscious mind.

The term which psychology has coined for our relative imperviousness to the dizzy variations that go on in the world around us is "constancy." The color, shape and brightness of things remain to us relatively constant, even though we may notice some variation with the change of distance, illumination, angle of vision, and so on. Our room remains the same room from dawn to midday to dusk, and the objects in it retain their shape and color. Only when we are faced with special tasks involving attention to these matters do we become aware of uncertainties. We would not judge the color of an unfamiliar fabric in artificial light, and we step into the middle of the room if we are asked whether a picture hangs straight on the wall.

Otherwise our capacity to make allowances, to infer from relationships alone, is astounding. We all know the experience at the cinema when we are ushered to a seat very far off-center. At first the screen and what is on it look so distorted and unreal that we feel like leaving. But in a few minutes we have learned to take our position into account, and the proportions right themselves. And as with shapes, so with colors. A faint light is disturbing at first, but with the aid of the physiological adaptation of the eye we soon get the feel of relationships, and the world assumes its familiar face.

Without this faculty of man and beast alike to recognize identities across the variations of difference, to make allowance for changed conditions, and to preserve the framework of a stable world, art could not exist.

8. The Natural World

On May 23, 1987, the *New York Times* ran a long obituary of Archie Carr, a zoologist who spent his entire fifty-five-year career studying the giant sea turtle. I had never heard of Professor Carr, but I enjoyed reading the story of his life. Operating mainly from a field camp in Costa Rica, he reestablished turtle populations in many countries where they had been almost exterminated for their food, developed tagging techniques that partly solved the mystery of their breeding cycle and their 1,200-mile migrations, and wrote eleven books that created a popular understanding of the work he and his colleagues were doing to save the species. (His academic base for all fifty-five years was the University of Florida at Gainesville.) Several of the books won literary awards and one of them, *The Windward Road,* inspired the formation of the Caribbean Conservation Corporation, a group that coordinates the research and rescue efforts that Professor Carr set in motion.

At first I found it incredible that a man would devote his whole life to one animal. But then I thought of my father, who died at ninety-one with his love undiminished for a business that made one product—the shellac business, William Zinsser & Co., that his German immigrant grandfather founded in 1849 and that was even nearer to extinction than the sea turtle when my father left college in 1909 to save it. To him the life cycle of the lac bug, spinning its resinous cocoon onto the twigs of trees north of Calcutta, was as romantic as the turtle's cycle obviously was to Archie Carr, and he brought to his work an enthusiasm and a passion for quality that made his business prosper. Seeing how much he enjoyed his work and how good he was at it, I learned at an early age what has been an important principle to me ever since—that what we want to do we will do well.

That principle would surely apply to Archie Carr, I thought, and I went out and got one of his books, *So Excellent a Fishe: A Natural History of Sea Turtles.* Its title comes from an act that was passed in 1620 by the Bermuda Assembly to stop "sundrye lewd & impvident psons who in their continuall goinges out to sea snatch & catch up indifferentlye all kinds of Tortoyses both yonge and old," thereby risking the extinction of "so excellent a fishe." I was delighted by the coincidence that delivered Professor Carr to me just as I was wondering what writers to include in a chapter on the natural world, though it really wasn't luck. Somebody said—I'm quite sure it wasn't me; it must have been Lord Chesterfield—that chance favors the prepared mind, and certainly it's true that writers, in some corner of their conscious or subconscious brain, are always working. A writer should always be ready to be lucky.

Enthusiasm, which I knew I would find in Archie Carr's book, is crucial to writing well. One reason I believe in writing-across-the-curriculum programs is that they encourage students to write about subjects that interest them, thus bringing them the surprising news that writing can be useful in their lives. It's astonishing how quickly high school students can learn to write if they want to get into college and need to compose an essay telling the admissions office why they are so desirable. All the aimlessness of their school papers—the lazy thinking, the clogged passages—is for one shining moment made tidy. Motivation clears the head faster than a nasal spray.

In Archie Carr's *So Excellent a Fishe* I was quickly caught up in the two central wonders of the sea turtle's life. One is that it is "among the spectacular animal travelers of the world," journeying with uncanny precision between Ascension Island and various Caribbean beaches by navigational methods that are still an enigma to science. The other is that at breeding time the three-hundred-pound female leaves the familiar safety of the sea and comes ashore to lay her eggs on hostile land. There she is both too ponderous and too preoccupied to put up a fight. "Once the nesting has started," Dr. Carr writes, "she will go on doggedly through the hour-long ceremony with a pack of dogs digging out her nest beneath her or with drunken Indians drumming on her back."

The number of eggs that she deposits under such discouraging conditions is itself one of nature's supreme measuring acts:

> When a green turtle comes ashore she lays roughly a hundred eggs. Compared to the number of eggs laid by wholly aquatic animals such as mackerel or lobsters, a hundred is not very many; but it is more than a lizard lays or a setting hen sets on. The biology [of that figure] is still mostly unknown, but it is clearly there. The whole race and destiny of the creature are probably balanced at the edge of limbo by the delicate weight of that magic number of eggs. One marvel of the number is how great it is; but another is, how small.

I like the casual purity of that sentence. It says everything it needs to say, and the word "marvel" gives it emotional weight, telling us that something remarkable is going on here. I know management consultants who can't talk about numbers without using the phrase "order of magnitude"; a six-pack of beer costs on an order of magnitude of five dollars.

> When you think of the unpromising future that confronts a turtle egg and the turtle hatchling that comes out of it, you wonder why sea turtles don't give up their stubborn, reckless

old ways of leaving their new generation on shore, and instead carry one big, well-tended egg in a pouch or release myriads of turtle larvae to join the plankton, and swamp the laws of chance with millions of largely expendable progeny. The answer, of course, is that the turtles have hit on the formula for outwitting predators, or at least for surviving in spite of them. The formula is simply one hundred turtle eggs. . . .

If you were able to get a complete list of the animals that prey on turtle eggs and young it would surely include most of the carnivores and omnivores, both vertebrate and invertebrate, that live near a turtle-nesting beach. The predators range in size from ants and crabs to bears. Some of them live along the beach itself, some in the coastal scrub. Some come from far back in the interior, showing up for the turtle season as the Siquirres dogs at Tortuguero used to do [Tortuguero is the site of Professor Carr's camp] and as the Rancho Nuevo coyotes do to this day.

At Tortuguero nowadays the most important non-human predators on the beach are dogs and buzzards. The dogs are the worst. They move in on a laying female and take the eggs as they are laid or prevent her from covering them. They are stronger at digging than buzzards are, too, though buzzards dig better than many people might imagine. Most people, in fact, probably don't imagine that buzzards dig at all. The other regular turtle eaters are opossums, the few domestic pigs that range the northernmost miles, and the ravening hosts of wari, or white-lipped peccaries, [which] sometimes travel out to the beach from the inland forest at nesting time and hatching time. This is of course a catastrophe, especially if it happens in early October when in hundreds of nests the little turtles rest in tight bundles in little cavities only an inch or less beneath the surface, waiting for the time that seems to them proper for bursting out into the unknown world. Wari are so devastating that when I am asked why the green turtle chooses Turtle Bogue to cling to, out of all the thousands of miles of Caribbean shore that look like good turtle beach, I think first of saying: because peccaries find it hard to get there across the lagoon. . . .

When [the hatchlings] do come out they waste no time about it. Their trip across the sand to the surf is both fast and direct. So for the turtles of each nest, this time of maximum peril in the whole life of the species is not really a long time at all. It is only a minute or two, or a little longer if the way to the sea should be blocked by many obstacles. Still it seems to a human observer a foolhardy violation of common sense to leave your young ones far back from the sea on the hungry shore, behind dunes or debris which (chances are) cut off the way to the sea and hide it from view. The little turtles come out into a world anxious to eat them. They have simply got to go fast and straight toward the ocean even though they can't see it, never saw it before, and know of its existence only as a set of signals to react to instinctively.

That's pleasant writing; we're there on the beach at Tortuguero, rooting for the turtles and hoping they won't meet a wari on their crawl to the surf. But the writing couldn't survive on charm alone; it works because it's grounded in scientific observation and fact. What sticks in our mind is the hundred eggs, the digging buzzards, the returning coyotes, the signaling sea. In fact, by the end of *So Excellent a Fishe* I knew more about sea turtles than I ever thought I wanted to know. I also enjoyed the trip, partly because the turtle ultimately gave up very few of its secrets—to Professor Carr or anyone else. Far from wondering how somebody could devote his whole life to one animal, I realized that it would take the fifty-five-year careers of platoons of scientists to determine how the turtle finds its way so unerringly across vast expanses of ocean.

I was also reminded that science in the hands of a good writer will have an unexpected human dimension. In this case the link is the tag that gets fastened to the turtle, requesting the finder to send it back to the University of Florida and to say where and when it was caught. Who are those finders? Professor Carr gives us a sampling of their replies. Most of them are fishermen and other coastal dwellers in remote villages and islands—people not in the habit of writing to professors of zoology. Yet they somehow understand the importance of what the man in Florida is trying to find out and are eager not to botch their brief role. The graciousness of their letters is one of the ornaments of the book:

> After saluting you affectionately I permit myself to communicate to you having captured a turtle with a metallic plaque which . . .

> I am a Miskito Indian from a small village named Dakura along the Miskito coast, to be able to remit this to you I was forced to come 15 miles to Puerto Cabezas, the closest point of communication . . .

> I am very glad to be the one that found this tyrtle drifting down to the Nicaraguan's water it was found in the Pear Lagoon bar on thursday 18 of August at 6:00 o'clock in the morning. I wish that I have explained every thing the right way . . .

> I am pleased to tell you that this turtle was catch at Marroon Cay by setting nets. I caught it on the 17 of Octobre of the passed year at 9:00 a.m. Nothing else for the moment, except I would like to keep in touch . . .

> Atentively I direct myself to you to send you a plaque that I found encrusted on a turtle that I caught on the coast of

Cojoro Venezuela. This demands that it be sent to your Institute. Receive a cordial embrace . . .

*

Unlike Archie Carr, who dropped into this book out of the blue, Charles Darwin is someone I knew I wanted to have along on the ride. The odds that he wouldn't be a good writer struck me as small—someone who gives the frontiers of knowledge an immense push is a good bet to be someone who can express his ideas clearly. Writing is the handmaiden of leadership; Abraham Lincoln and Winston Churchill rode to glory on the back of the strong declarative sentence. I can't claim, however, that my theory is watertight; it gets shipwrecked, for instance, on the rocky prose of Buckminster Fuller, and Fuller is by no means the only innovative thinker whose thoughts spill out in majestic disarray.

Fortunately, Darwin didn't let me down. Two pages were enough to prove my hunch. I bought a copy of his *The Voyage of the Beagle* and started right in:

After having been twice driven back by heavy south-western gales, Her Majesty's ship *Beagle,* a ten-gun brig, under the command of Captain Fitz Roy, R. N., sailed from Devonport on the 27th of December, 1831. The object of the expedition was to complete the survey of Patagonia and Tierra del Fuego, commenced under Captain King in 1826 to 1830—to survey the shores of Chile, Peru, and some islands in the Pacific—and to carry a chain of chronometrical measurements round the world. On the 6th of January we reached Teneriffe, but were prevented landing, by fears of our bringing the cholera: the next morning we saw the sun rise behind the rugged outline of the Grand Canary island, and suddenly illumine the Peak of Teneriffe, whilst the lower parts were veiled in fleecy clouds. This was the first of many delightful days never to be forgotten. On the 16th of January, 1832, we anchored at Porto Praya, in St. Jago, the chief island of the Cape de Verd archipelago.

The many delightful days would stretch to four years and nine months before the *Beagle* would touch England again, and the voyage would revolutionize man's view of his position in the natural order. But here Charles Darwin is just a young man, twenty-two years old, who signed on as ship's naturalist because he thought it would be an opportunity for "collecting, observing and noting anything worthy to be noted in natural history."

His first paragraph did the necessary work of telling us why the expedition was formed. The second one lets us know instantly that this is no ordinary observer:

The neighborhood of Porto Praya, viewed from the sea, wears a desolate aspect. The volcanic fires of a past age, and the scorching heat of a tropical sun, have in most places rendered the soil unfit for vegetation. The country rises in successive steps of table-land, interspersed with some truncate conical hills, and the horizon is bounded by an irregular chain of more lofty mountains. The scene, as beheld through the hazy atmosphere of this climate, is one of great interest; if, indeed, a person, fresh from the sea, and who has just walked, for the first time, in a grove of cocoa-nut trees, can be a judge of anything but his own happiness. The island would generally be considered as very uninteresting; but to any one accustomed only to an English landscape, the novel aspect of an utterly sterile land possesses a grandeur which any more vegetation might spoil. A single green leaf can scarcely be discovered over wide tracts of the lava plains; yet flocks of goats, together with a few cows, contrive to exist.

So unendingly rich is *The Voyage of the Beagle* in its accounts of animals, birds and the whole panoply of natural life that I could quote from any of its five hundred pages. I've chosen the following episode because it takes place in the Galapagos archipelago, which was of course the expedition's pivotal landfall, enabling Darwin, because of the long isolation of those islands from nature's chain, to study animal forms that didn't exist anywhere else and thus to glimpse his theory of the origin of species and the survival of the fittest.

It is now the fall of 1835; the *Beagle* has been at sea for almost four years. But Darwin has lost none of his reportorial zest as he describes a lizard that even he seems to regard as one of evolution's oddballs:

> The Amblyrhynchus, a remarkable genus of lizards, is con-
> fined to this archipelago. There are two species, resembling
> each other in general form, one being terrestrial and the other
> aquatic. The latter species (A. cristatus) was first characterized
> by Mr. Bell, who well foresaw from its short, broad head, and
> strong claws of equal length, that its habits of life would turn
> out very peculiar, and different from those of its nearest ally,
> the Iguana. It is extremely common on all the islands through-
> out the group, and lives exclusively on the rocky sea-beaches,
> being never found, at least I never saw one, even ten yards
> in-shore. It is a hideous-looking creature, of a dirty black color,
> stupid, and sluggish in its movements. The usual length of a
> full-grown one is about a yard, but there are some even four
> feet long; a large one weighed twenty pounds.
>
> Their tails are flattened sideways, and all four feet partially
> webbed. They are occasionally seen some hundred yards from
> shore, swimming about.... This lizard swims with perfect ease
> and quickness, by a serpentine movement of its body and
> flattened tail—the legs being motionless and closely collapsed
> on its sides. A seaman on board sank one, with a heavy weight
> attached to it, thinking thus to kill it directly; but when, an
> hour afterwards, he drew up the line, it was quite active. Their
> limbs and strong claws are admirably adapted for crawling

over the rugged and fissured masses of lava, which everywhere form the coast. In such situations, a group of six or seven
of these hideous reptiles may oftentimes be seen on the black
rocks, a few feet above the surf, basking in the sun with outstretched legs.

I opened the stomachs of several and found them distended
with minced sea-weed (Ulvae), which grows in thin foliaceous
expansions of bright green or a dull red color. I do not recollect
having observed this sea-weed in any quantity on the tidal
rocks; and I have reason to believe it grows at the bottom of
the sea, at some little distance from the coast. If such be the
case, the object of these animals occasionally going out to sea
is explained. The stomach contained nothing but the sea-
weed. Mr. Bynoe, however, found a piece of a crab in one; but
this might have got in accidentally, in the same manner as I
have seen a caterpillar, in the midst of some lichen, in the
paunch of a tortoise.

Notice how welcome it is to hear about human activity in the
midst of so much scientific activity. Darwin keeps reminding us
that this is an expedition and that science is done by people,
usually in collaboration. The references to Mr. Bell, who first
surmised that the lizard would turn out very peculiar; to Mr.
Bynoe, who evidently was just as inquisitive as Darwin about
the contents of its stomach, and to the seaman who found the
lizard "quite active" after sinking it for an hour with a weight—
these vignettes give us a sense of being along on the *Beagle*'s
voyage. We get a feeling for the dailiness of scientific research:
the steady accretion of facts about the lizards basking on the
beach but not venturing ten yards inland ("at least I never saw
one"). Caught up in the general curiosity, we're eager to learn
what else Darwin found out about this unlovely specimen.

The intestines were large, as in other herbivorous animals.
The nature of this lizard's food, as well as the structure of its

tail and feet, and the fact of its having been seen voluntarily swimming out at sea, absolutely prove its aquatic habits; yet there is in this respect one strange anomaly, namely, that when frightened it will not enter the water. Hence it is easy to drive these lizards down to any little point overhanging the sea, where they will sooner allow a person to catch hold of their tails than jump into the water. They do not seem to have any notion of biting; but when much frightened they squirt a drop of fluid from each nostril. I threw one several times as far as I could, into a deep pool left by the retiring tide; but it invariably returned in a direct line to the spot where I stood. It swam near the bottom, with a very graceful and rapid movement, and occasionally aided itself over the uneven ground with its feet. As soon as it arrived near the edge, but still being under water, it tried to conceal itself in the tufts of sea-weed, or it entered some crevice. As soon as it thought the danger was past, it crawled out on the dry rocks and shuffled away as quickly as it could.

I several times caught this same lizard, by driving it down to a point, and though possessed of such perfect powers of diving and swimming, nothing would induce it to enter the water; and as often as I threw it in, it returned in the manner above described. Perhaps this singular piece of apparent stupidity may be accounted for by the circumstance that this reptile has no enemy whatever on shore, whereas at sea it must often fall a prey to the numerous sharks. Hence, probably, urged by a fixed and hereditary instinct that the shore is its place of safety, whatever the emergency may be, it there takes refuge. . . .

I asked several of the inhabitants if they knew where it laid its eggs; they said that they knew nothing of its propagation, although well acquainted with the eggs of the land kind—a fact, considering how very common this lizard is, not a little extraordinary.

That's the writing of a scientist totally committed to his subject. But Darwin never forgets that the purpose of his writing is to transmit information. *The Voyage of the Beagle* is above all supremely useful—which is its supreme strength. Nonfiction writing should always have a point: It should leave the reader with a set of facts, or an idea, or a point of view, that he didn't have before he started reading. Writers may write for any number of good personal reasons—ego, therapy, recollection, validation of their lives. But what they produce will have a validity of its own to the extent that it's useful to somebody else.

It's not necessary to be Darwin, however, to write helpfully about the natural world. There's plenty of important writing to be done about the animals, fish and birds in our own increasingly crowded habitat. I'm a fan, for instance, of a magazine called *Missouri Conservationist*, which performs the genial tightrope act of telling the people of Missouri both how to enjoy their state and how to take care of it. Its articles aren't shrill or punitive; they never say: "Don't hunt and don't fish." What they do say is: "Be informed. Know the facts." The following passage is from an article by Tom R. Johnson, a herpetologist, which tries to allay the "needless anxiety and fear" associated with water snakes:

> Water snakes are often classed as "pugnacious" by people who have tried to capture them. As with many forms of wildlife, these snakes will not hesitate to defend themselves. If grabbed by a person, a water snake will thrash about violently, reach around and bite, and also smear a foul-smelling musk from glands in the base of the tail. Contrary to popular belief, water snakes can and do bite while underwater, either to defend themselves or to catch prey. In all cases, however, the bite caused by a water snake produces mild scratches and nothing more.
>
> What do water snakes eat? I wish more people would ask

this question before killing water snakes. Many people have the mistaken idea that these animals eat too many fish and are not good for anything. Some people who fish look upon water snakes as competitors for game fish and try to kill every snake they see. Just the opposite is true. Water snakes predominantly eat nongame fish—especially diseased or injured ones. A number of studies have shown that water snakes pose no threat to fish populations or to our sport fisheries. They add to the aquatic environment both as predator and prey. Besides fish, water snakes eat frogs and tadpoles, salamanders and crayfish. Young water snakes are food for bass, pickerel, goggle-eye, bullfrogs, mink, otter and herons.

Another reason why people who fish do not enjoy seeing water snakes is that they think these snakes are aggressive. I have had people tell me about snakes that "came right after them" or that "tried to get into their boat." This does actually happen, but not because of aggression. Water snakes locate their prey—diseased or injured fish—by smell. An injured fish gives off an odor that is quickly picked up by a water snake's tongue. A successful fisherman, surrounded by the odor of injured fish, may find himself in the company of a hungry snake with one thing on its mind: "Where's the fish?" This is not aggression; it is a reaction to a possible food source. The snake is just doing its job as predator or scavenger and is not after the person fishing.

*

But (I hear you saying) can't we please have some ordinary animals? Cows, maybe. Or pigs. Fair enough—most of us get through our allotted span without running into a water snake, a giant sea turtle or an Amblyrhynchus cristatus. So I'll conclude with two forms of natural life that there's no getting away from: insects and birds.

In the literature of insects one name towers over all others:

the French entomologist J. Henri Fabre. That's my main reason
for including him here—it's always a pleasure to see giants at
work. But I have two further reasons. One has to do with translation. Because Fabre was French, his work raises the question
of what qualities enable writing to cross over into another language. My other reason has to do with drive. Because of the
astonishing curve of Fabre's career he should be the patron
saint of all those people who say they'd "like to try a little
writing sometime" when they retire from the boring job
they're doing now.

Born in 1823, the son of peasants in Provence, Fabre spent
the bulk of his life in poverty, piecing together academic odd
jobs—teaching and writing instructional science books—that
barely supported him and his family. On Thursday afternoons,
the traditional half-day of French education, and on summer
holidays he studied the insect world. Not until he was fifty-five
had he saved enough money to buy his first piece of land—an
arid tract outside the village of Sérignan, which was unfit for
grazing or agriculture but ideal for wasps, wild bees and other
insects that he wanted to study and write about for the remainder of his days. Thus began his monumental work, *Souvenirs
Entomologiques,* which would take him twenty-eight years to
complete. Its ten volumes attracted so little attention as they
periodically came off the press that nobody could have foreseen
how the long saga would finally end.

As Edwin Way Teale tells the story in the introduction to his
anthology *The Insect World of J. Henri Fabre:* "His long years
of neglect, his decades of painstaking labor, ended in five exhausting years of fame. Fabre was eighty-four when the last of
the ten volumes of his magnum opus appeared. Soon after-
wards, he was suddenly discovered by such eminent literary
figures as Maurice Maeterlinck, Edmond Rostand and Romain
Rolland. A jubilee in his honor was held at Sérignan in 1910.
Government officials and representatives of scientific institu-

tions and societies did him homage. A statue was erected in the village. People who had never heard of the 'Insect's Homer' began reading his books at home and abroad. Scientific societies in London, Brussels, Stockholm, Geneva and St. Petersburg elected him to membership. The government bestowed upon him an annual pension of $400. The president of France journeyed to Sérignan to meet its first citizen. After the long years of poverty, of labor, of niggardly recognition, Fabre, nearing his ninetieth year, saw with his failing eyesight the sunshine of brilliant acclaim."

That his writing could make friends in so many countries, surviving the usual perils of translation, was no accident. "I have always thought that the quality of being readily rendered into a foreign tongue is a test of good writing," said the translator of Fabre's works into English, Alexander Teixeira de Mattos. "It is the tortured, labored, fantastic, would-be 'original' style that hampers the translator. Fabre's style is invariably straightforward."

What had formed the straightforward style was the discipline of cranking out textbooks that popularized science by presenting it to students in prose that was both simple and interesting. It was writing that paid the bills and taught Fabre a craft. Later, when he could at last turn to the work that had been in his heart all along, he added the priceless gift of enthusiasm—an ingredient mentioned in this book with shameless frequency. He also brought the gift of his personality, one that took me by surprise with its warmth and humor; somehow I had never connected the words "charm" and "entomologist." My interest in insects has been always minimal and often adversarial—the mosquito and the hornet and the cockroach have seen to that. But my interest in Fabre's interest in insects is high. The transaction between a writer and his subject is the central relationship in nonfiction.

Here's how one of Fabre's chapters begins:

Among the treasures of my laboratory I place in the first rank an ant-hill of *Polyergus rufescens,* the celebrated Red Ant, the slave-hunting Amazon. Unable to rear her family, incapable of seeking her food, of taking it even when it is within her reach, she needs servants who feed her and undertake the duties of housekeeping. The Red Ants make a practice of stealing children to wait on the community. They ransack the neighboring ant-hills, the home of a different species; they carry away nymphs, which soon attain maturity in the strange house and become willing and industrious servants.

When the hot weather of June and July sets in, I often see the Amazons leave their barracks of an afternoon and start on an expedition. The column measures five or six yards in length. If nothing worthy of attention be met upon the road, the ranks are fairly well maintained; but, at the first suspicion of an ant-hill, the vanguard halts and deploys in a swarming throng. Scouts are sent out; the Amazons recognize that they are on a wrong track; and the column forms again. It resumes its march, crosses the garden paths, disappears from sight in the grass, reappears farther on, threads its way through the heaps of dead leaves, comes out again and continues its search. At last, a nest of Black Ants is discovered. The Red Ants hasten down to the dormitories where the nymphs lie and soon emerge with their booty. Then we have, at the gates of the underground city, a bewildering scrimmage between the defending blacks and the attacking reds. The struggle is too unequal to remain indecisive. Victory falls to the reds, who race back to their abode, each with her prize, a swaddled nymph, dangling from her mandibles.

Obviously Fabre has been well served by his translator, De Mattos, a man sensitive to language and rhythm and to the nuance that prefers a particular word to its near neighbor. But even a poor translator couldn't kill a style that moves with such narrative certainty. Fabre is telling us the story of a raid; he could be talking about the Comanches swooping down on Fort Dodge. The return trip is no less vivid:

> The route taken [on the raid] is a matter of indifference to the marching column. Bare ground, thick grass, a heap of dead leaves or stone, brickwork, a clump of shrubs: all are crossed without any marked preference for one sort of road rather than another. What is rigidly fixed is the path home, which follows the outward track in all its windings and all its crossings, however difficult. Laden with their plunder, the Red Ants return to the nest by the same road, often an exceedingly complicated one, which the exigencies of the chase compelled them to take originally. They repass each spot which they passed at first; and this is to them a matter of such imperative necessity that no additional fatigue nor even the gravest danger can make them alter the track.

"Can you give us an example?" we think at this point. A good writer always knows what his readers are thinking and what they want to be told next. Fabre nails down the general principle with a specific case:

> Let us suppose that they have crossed a thick heap of dead leaves, representing to them a path beset with yawning gulfs, where every moment some one falls, where many are exhausted as they struggle out of the hollows and reach the heights by means of swaying bridges, emerging at last from the labyrinth of lanes. No matter: on their return they will not fail, though weighed down with their burden, once more to struggle through that weary maze. To avoid all this fatigue, they would have but to swerve slightly from the original path, for the good, smooth road is there, hardly a step away. This little deviation never occurs to them.

I came upon them one day when they were on one of their raids. They were marching along the inner edge of the stone-work of the garden pond, where I have replaced the old batra-chians [frogs and toads] by a colony of goldfish. The wind was blowing very hard from the north and, taking the column in flank, sent whole rows of the ants flying into the water. The fish hurried up; they watched the performance and gobbled up the drowning insects. It was a difficult bit; and the column was decimated before it had passed. I expected to see the return journey made by another road, which would wind round and avoid the fatal cliff. Not at all. The nymph-laden band resumed the parlous path and the goldfish received a double windfall: the ants and their prizes. Rather than alter its track, the col-umn was decimated a second time.

I can't leave Fabre without turning him loose briefly on the firefly, or glow-worm, that blithe diversion of our summer nights. How does a mere insect do something so ingratiating? Here's how Fabre introduces him:

Few insects vie in popular fame with the glow-worm, that curious little animal which, to celebrate the little joys of life, kindles a beacon at its tail-end. Who does not know it, at least by name? Who has not seen it roam amid the grass, like a spark fallen from the moon at its full? The Greeks of old called it λαμπομρις, meaning the bright-tailed. Science employs the same term: it calls the lantern-bearer *Lampyris noctiluca*. In this case, the common name is inferior to the scientific phrase, which, when translated, becomes both expressive and accu-rate.

In fact, we might easily cavil at the word "worm." The Lampyris is not a worm at all, not even in general appearance. He has six short legs, which he well knows how to use; he is a gad-about, a trot-about. In the adult state, the male is correctly garbed in wing-cases, like the true Beetle that he is. The female is an ill-favored thing who knows naught of the delights of flying: all her life long she retains the larval shape. [But] even in this initial stage, the word "worm" is out of place. We French have the expression "naked as a worm," to point to the lack of any defensive covering. Now the Lampyris is clothed, that is to say, he wears an epidermis of some consistency; moreover, he is rather richly colored: his body is dark brown all over, set off with pale pink on the thorax, especially on the lower surface. Finally, each segment is decked at the hinder edge with two spots of a fairly bright red. A costume like this was never worn by a worm.

Having rescued the glow-worm from wormdom, Fabre invokes the words of his compatriot, the gastronome Henri Brillat-Savarin, who said, "Show me what you eat and I will tell you what you are." A similar question, Fabre says, "should be addressed to every insect whose habits we propose to study, for, from the least to the greatest in the zoological progression, the stomach sways the world; the data supplied by food are the chief of all the documents of life." He proceeds to tell us that the seemingly docile firefly is in fact "a hunter of game [who] follows his calling with rare villainy. His regular prey is the snail. Before he begins to feast, the glow-worm administers an anesthetic: he chloroforms his victim, rivaling in the process the wonders of our modern surgery."

Six pages later Fabre has taken us through two bizarre procedures: an intricate feat of anesthesia and an act of gastronomy so fastidious that it wouldn't be out of place at Brillat-Savarin's table, concluding with "a wash and brush-up," which the glow-worm performs "point by point, from one end of the body to the other, with a scrupulous persistency that proves the great interest which he takes in the operation. What is his object in thus sponging himself, in dusting and polishing himself so carefully? It is a question, apparently, of removing a few atoms of dust or else some traces of viscidity that remain from the evil contact with the snail."

Only then does Fabre get around to explaining what most of us thought was the firefly's real parlor trick:

> If the glow-worm possessed no other talent than that of chloroforming his prey by means of a few tweaks resembling kisses, he would be unknown to the vulgar herd. But he also knows how to light himself like a beacon; he shines, which is an excellent manner of achieving fame. . . .

Surely, we might think, nobody would ever write so well about the insect world again. But in our own time one writer, Vladimir Nabokov, has matched Fabre for elegance. Nabokov's obsession, which began when he was a child in Russia, touched only one small corner of Fabre's universe: butterflies and moths. But the intensity with which it bobs up in his writing is proof of how it consumed him.

English was Nabokov's fourth language, but no native-born writer of my native language dazzles me more with the precision of his imagery. Though the hilarious *Lolita* is a work of fiction, it's one of the most minutely observed travel books ever written about America and its tacky landscape of motels and burger huts. Nabokov's exactitude reaches its purest refinement in *Speak, Memory,* that most stylish of memoirs. In the following excerpt he recalls how his "ardent adolescent interest" led him to ponder "the links between butterflies and the central problems of nature."

> The mysteries of mimicry had a special attraction for me. Its phenomena showed an artistic perfection usually associated with man-wrought things. Such was the imitation of oozing poison by bubble-like macules on a wing (complete with

pseudo-refraction) or by glossy yellow knobs on a chrysalis ("Don't eat me—I have already been squashed, sampled and rejected"). When a certain moth resembled a certain wasp in shape and color, it also walked and moved its antennae in a waspish, un-mothlike manner. When a butterfly had to look like a leaf, not only were all the details of a leaf beautifully rendered but markings mimicking grub-bored holes were generously thrown in. "Natural selection," in the Darwinian sense, could not explain the miraculous coincidence of imitative aspect and imitative behavior, nor could one appeal to the theory of "the struggle for life" when a protective device was carried to a point of mimetic subtlety, exuberance and luxury far in excess of a predator's power of appreciation. I discovered in nature the non-utilitarian delights that I sought in art. Both were a form of magic, both were a game of intricate enchantment and deception.

*

Finally, birds. Though nobody has ever confused me with Roger Tory Peterson, I often marvel at certain prodigies of bird behavior—flight, song, nest-building, migration—that seem to me beyond explaining. At such times I turn to a book called *Birds and Their Attributes,* by Glover Morrill Allen. The book was published in 1925, but I doubt if anyone knows more about birds today than Professor Allen knew then—typical chapters are "Feathers," "Birds' Colors and Their Uses" and "Bills, Feet, Wings, and Bones"—or can write about their habits with such clarity and vigor. Here's how he explains the attribute of birds that man has envied and tried to emulate since Icarus flew too near the sun:

We do not know how birds first became fliers, but it is supposed that their early ancestors ran on their hind legs, leaving their fore limbs free to develop as wings or as sails by the aid of which they glided from bough to bough or from tree to tree. In this the wings were probably held outstretched and the legs were extended behind. In many bats additional support is gained by the growth of a membrane which stretches between the extended toes and the tip of the tail. This is called a "patagium."

With "patagium" Professor Allen throws a technical term at us from his discipline of zoology. That's the prerogative of any writer writing about a special field, and as educated readers we should be glad to know about such strangers and to make them our own. I'm delighted to meet "patagium." But a writer also has an obligation to make us comfortable with these terms, not to use them unnecessarily or just to show off or to exclude everyone who isn't a member of the lodge. Here Professor Allen takes the time to explain why the word is important to the point he is making:

It has been argued that if the ancestors of birds had learned to glide before their feathery covering had become evolved, they would probably have had a thin membrane of skin stretching between the fingers and from the sides of the tail to the feet, just as there is in bats and in the extinct flying lizards or pterodactyls. Since, however, this "patagium" is lacking, it is believed that some of the feathers on the hand had already become large enough to sustain the bird in the air.

That ancient birds extended the legs *behind* in flight is rendered probable not only from analogy with bats, but also because most of the primitive birds still do so. For example, ducks, loons, herons, cranes, sandpipers, gulls, as well as grouse, hens, hawks, owls, pigeons and the cuckoos all fly with the legs out behind when under way, in contrast to many of the more specialized or perching birds which fly with the feet drawn up in front ready to grasp a branch on alighting; such are the crows, sparrows, warblers, thrushes. . . .

After the gliding stage, flight was perhaps acquired by a laborious process of alternate flapping and sailing, much as we see in the Sharp-shinned Hawk when not in direct flight. The primitive flying birds were probably small species and by gradually increasing the rapidity of their wing beats they developed swifter flight. Observations made in Europe on birds harnessed to automatic registers showed in the pigeon about 480 wing beats to the minute, in a duck 540, and in the sparrow 780. . . .

Once the art of sustaining the body in air was acquired, we may suppose the more expert forms of flight followed, such as soaring, or poising with delicate adjustment on air currents. Such a form of poising is seen in the Rough-legged Hawks, which have learned to hang in the air nearly motionless by balancing on an upward current coming over the brow of a hill. . . .

Professor Allen is on a roll here that any sportswriter might envy. One of the hardest kinds of writing is to describe motion in a way that the reader can picture. Dance critics also know the problem. Specific detail, as always, helps:

Passengers on steamers have often admired the beautiful flight of gulls which, taking advantage of the wave of air forced upward by the advance of the vessel against the wind, are able to poise on motionless wings in this current and yet keep pace with the steamer as it advances. Once outside a certain zone, however, the force of the air current falls and they cannot maintain their position except by flapping. These two cases indicate a very delicate adjustment of forces in the poising bird.

But even this feat of equilibrium is not the most glorious of the flying arts, as Professor Allen, leading us from the simple to the intricate, as good teachers and nonfiction writers should, goes on to explain:

> The most complex and interesting type of flight is true soaring, by which is meant the ability to glide through the air, to rise or descend, to increase or check speed, to circle or go straight away, all without flapping the wings or greatly varying the general outstretched position. . . .
>
> In calm air there is very little drift down wind, but instead the successive circles overlap. There may be circling without gain in height—or "ease-circling." With an increase of wind the circles may overlap less and less, making loops to leeward, and there often comes a sudden increase of speed at the commencement of the down-wind glide, following a slight adjustment of the wings.
>
> In "ease-circling" without gain of height the wings are held straight out from the shoulder. In gliding straight ahead, however, there is a slight bend at the wrist which advances the primary feathers of the wings nearly to the level of the beak. This gives greater speed and is called "flex-gliding."
>
> Soaring flight does not occur at any or all times. On the contrary, in calm air, soaring flight may not be possible in early morning or late afternoon, but as morning advances its occurrence depends upon the presence of upward currents of air due to the heating of the lowermost layers of the atmosphere. In other words, the air becomes "soarable" at a more or less particular time, and this "soarability" gradually increases, as proved by the fact that the lighter birds first start circling and the heavier ones follow in the order of their weight.

Professor Allen isn't bad at soarability himself.

9. Writing Mathematics

One day I got a letter from a woman named Joan Country-man, who is head of the mathematics department at German-town Friends School in Philadelphia. She had heard about my interest in writing across the curriculum.

"For many years," she said, "I've been asking my students to write about mathematics as they learned it, with predictably wonderful results. Writing seems to free them of the idea that math is a collection of right answers owned by the teacher—a body of knowledge that she will dispense in chunks and that they have to swallow and digest. That's how most non-mathematicians perceive it. But what makes mathematics really interesting is not the right answer but where it came from and where it leads."

The letter grabbed my attention. Surely mathematics was a world of numbers. Could it also be penetrated with words? Could a person actually write sentences that would lead him through a mathematical problem and suggest further questions—different questions from the ones the teacher might raise? It had never occurred to me that the teacher wasn't the sole custodian of mathematical truth, and it certainly never occurred to E. Grant Spicer, my elementary school math teacher, who so cowed me with his ownership of the right answer that I've had math anxiety ever since. To this day I consider it a lucky month when I balance my checkbook, and the task is always accompanied by a slight pounding in my chest that I would otherwise take to be the onset of a heart attack. I still resent having to subtract a larger number from a smaller one by "borrowing" from the adjacent column. I resent it not only because I'm never sure I've done it right; I also seem to have to borrow more often than anyone else does. Why me?

Such self-pity would have been despised by Mr. Spicer; emotions have no place in mathematics. He was one of those people who have "a head for figures," instantly certain that twelve times nine is—well, whatever it is. Confronted with a student who was unable to produce the right answer, he would begin to turn red, a man betrayed by his vascular system, until his round face and bald head were crimson with disbelief that such dim-wittedness was at large in the next generation. After my years under his baleful gaze I took as little math as possible, banishing it along with chemistry to the limbo of subjects I didn't think I had an aptitude for.

Yet here in the morning mail was a teacher who got her math students to write—a humanist in the world of fractions and cosines. Joan Countryman explained that she was one of a small but growing number of pioneers in her discipline, frequently invited to give workshops to introduce teachers to the idea of writing mathematics. I called her and asked if she would introduce the idea to me. My palms were so sweaty that I could hardly hold the phone—a condition that AT&T's long lines obviously transmitted. The woman I was calling could tell she had a mathophobe on her hands. "I know I can help you," she said.

We made a date for me to come to Philadelphia and talk to her and attend one of her classes.

*

I put my first question to Joan Countryman as we settled down to talk in her late-Victorian house, a house I had been warmly admiring for its fanciful curves and angles and other eclectic design details.

"What is mathematics?" I asked.

"You've been talking about mathematics ever since you walked into this house," she said. "When you commented on the dormers and the staircase and the circular windows you were making mathematical points."

I said I thought they were aesthetic points. Like Molière's bourgeois gentleman, who was astonished to learn that he had been speaking prose all his life, I was surprised to learn that I had been speaking mathematics.

"Sure they're aesthetic points," she said, "but there are all sorts of interesting mathematics about the way the house is constructed and about the shapes you've been noticing. Unfortunately, most people don't see the world that way because they've been alienated from mathematics and told that it's something apart from what they're able to do."

"So what is mathematics?" I asked, still hoping for a definition.

"What are any of the disciplines but a way in which people try to make sense of the world or the universe?" she said. "Mathematics is one way of doing that, just as literature is, or philosophy, or history. Math does it by looking for patterns and abstracting—that is, by examining a specific case and generalizing from that. But that's not how a child would define mathematics. He'd say that math is arithmetic—adding and subtracting and multiplying and dividing—because that's the first thing we make him do. We spend far too much time on it; today we've got calculators that can do the job faster and better. I don't think we should even teach long division anymore; kids spend so much time learning to do it, and getting it wrong, that they never see the point of it—why you would *want* to do it. But with a calculator doing the drudgery, you can ask an interesting question, like 'How much fabric do I need to cover this chair?' "

"When you ask a question about the fabric does it become something beyond arithmetic?" I asked.

"It does, because you begin to make connections. Unless you make those connections, children will always think of mathematics as somehow 'other than me—not part of my world.' And that continues right through high school, where there's a heavy emphasis on exercises and computation, with numbers as the sole language and the right answer as the sole objective."

I asked Joan Countryman when she began to think that there might be another language—writing—which could take students into the subject by a different route.

"When I started teaching math I was thirty," she recalled, "and I had been out working in the field of urban education as a program planner for the Philadelphia school district, so when I got into a classroom I had serious questions about the relationship between what one does in school and what one does in life. I didn't like the isolation of the process of learning math: You study it alone and you take your tests alone and you don't have much to do with other people. I immediately put the kids in groups and made them teach each other and take tests together. I was determined to get them away from the idea that their education is a private experience.

"I also wanted them to be less passive. Math is an active process, and you'll never know that if you sit and wait for the teacher to tell you, 'This is how to do long division—it's a set of specific steps.' The action should begin long before that, with the student initiating a question like 'I've got fifty-three of these things; how am I going to divide them among the people in the room?' Most kids think that the teacher has all the information and they don't have any. I don't like the implications of that— that you aren't capable of finding things out yourself.

"So from the start I got my students to write about what they were doing. My first idea was to ask them to write mathematics autobiographies. That's when I realized there was some amaz-

ing stuff in their heads. They had very specific memories of
their classroom experiences. It wasn't just: 'I don't like math';
it was: 'In the middle of the third grade when Miss Thompson
made me do that sheet with the 100 additions I felt terrible
because I couldn't get it right.' They conveyed a strong sense
of what it was like to be in a math classroom. Many of them told
wonderful stories; in fact, some of the kids who were most
enthusiastic weren't particularly good at math. What those autobiographies did was to remind me that I wasn't teaching
empty vessels—that these people had long histories of mathematics even though they were only thirteen. I saw that it was
possible for me to be in touch with them."

Still, writing about math isn't the same thing as writing math.
I asked Mrs. Countryman how she made the crucial next step:
from writing as recollection to writing to learn. She said she
began encouraging her students to think of math topics they
could explore in writing.

"One of my favorites," she said, "was a student who has since
become a professional tennis player. He said, 'Do you really
mean I could study the geometry of the tennis court?' He wrote
a paper that analyzed the serve and discussed various issues that
he discovered as he wrote about them. Mainly he was noticing
that mathematics was involved in what he was doing on the
tennis court—a connection he had never made before because
he was math-handicapped. He was the kind of person who said,
'Math isn't for me.'"

Whether the student also improved his serve I didn't ask. A
different question was on my mind: "Are there things you can
find out by writing about a math problem that you can't learn
by mathematics alone? Or would a math whiz know everything
he needed to know by the conventional methods?"

"That's the question that worried me most when I started,"
Mrs. Countryman said. "The students I was frightened of—
wary of—were the hotshot math kids who were sure they didn't

want to do any writing or would consider it a waste of time. But even those kids are eventually saying to me, 'This is really useful. I'm learning mathematics better because I'm writing this stuff.' "

*

I needed to see some examples of what we were talking about. Joan Countryman began by showing me two pieces of writing elicited by the question: "Find a number with thirteen factors." Her usual procedure, she said, is to pose a problem to the class, lead a discussion of it and ask the students to write about it in this format: (1) Describe the problem; (2) Discuss your approach; (3) Explain what you found out.

The first example, by a seventh-grade boy named Francis Vargas, was in the form of a letter—a device Mrs. Countryman invented because "math students often find it easier to write about their work when they're writing to a specific person." Francis's letter began like this:

Dear Jim:

In math class we had a problem which was to find a number that had thirteen factors. At first we tried it by guessing, but it seemed hopeless. Then we made a list which included squares of numbers up to twenty and the factors of the numbers, and at the end we counted the factors. From that we saw that the squares that had three factors had square roots that were prime. Then we made a list like the one below.... From that list we saw that when the numbers were doubled we noticed a consecutive sequence starting from two in the column that showed the number of factors....

Proceeding with narrative logic, Francis needed only a few more sentences to tell Jim how he found the missing number.

"Writing is a way to explore a question and gain control over it," Mrs. Countryman said. "But it also engages the imagination, the intellect and the emotions, and these are powerful aids to learning." True enough, I thought—at least in most subjects. But could that apply to math? The next paper answered my question. Written by a seventh grader named Ian Childs, it came at the problem of the thirteen factors from a strikingly different direction:

THE THIRTEENTH FACTOR

As I sat in my office on Saturday morning waiting for a case, suddenly a sharp knock came upon my door.

"Come in," I called.

The door opened slowly and in came a man with a long overcoat and hat. A shadow was cast over his face. He walked slowly up to my desk and dropped an envelope on it.

"Read," he said.

I read, "TOP SECRET GOVERNMENT INFORMATION: Find a number with 13 factors or the world is . . ." Suddenly the paper burned up. I imagined that it was supposed to self-destruct after a certain period of time.

"Do you accept?" he asked.

"Yes."

"Good. Begin work immediately." He turned, began to walk out the door and said, "and swiftly."

I soon realized that the number had to be a perfect square, perfect squares being the only numbers with an odd number of factors since the square root would pair off with itself. The number's square root could not be a prime because all numbers squared from a prime would have three and only three factors.

Should I list every square number? No, too long and too much work. I've got it!! The perfect way! Why didn't I think of it before? I will list all the numbers that are power of two, and the one to the twelfth power will have to have 13 factors!

Conclusion: the number 4096 was the one with 13 factors and I returned it to the government. What part it played in saving the world I don't know, but I'm still here today. I learned many things from this case, like how to find a number with any amount of factors and how to get a number with three factors (a prime^2).

Another format is for students to keep a journal with a running account of their work. "In a journal," Mrs. Countryman said, "I want them to suspend judgment—to feel free to ask questions, to experiment, to make statements about what they do and don't understand. At first they need help to learn to write without censoring their thoughts—to feel confident that nobody will criticize what they've written."

The following entry, written by a twelfth-grade student named Neil Swenson after a month's exposure to calculus, is typical of how the form lends itself to recording successive stages of thought:

In my first journal entry I wrote that I believed that calculus is a way of finding solutions to problems that can't be solved with conventional math, by using abstractions. I was partially correct in that many parts of calculus do require abstract thinking. But that's not really what calculus is. Calculus is a way of dealing with motion. It's a way of finding out exactly how something is moving. Without calculus it was impossible for us to know what the instantaneous velocity of something was. We could only know the actual rate of change if it was changing at a constant rate; then its derivative or the slope of its tangent line is equal to the slope of the original line. When we had something that had a variable rate of exchange we tried to find the average velocity, but this was inaccurate.

I wondered whether Neil and Ian were both versions of my own teen-age self—boys whose main aptitude was for writing—and whether I might also have been able to write my way toward the thirteen-factor number and the instantaneous velocity of a moving object. Or was the whole matter of aptitudes a myth—a cop-out used by people like me to avoid subjects that would force us to think in new and therefore threatening ways? I asked Joan Countryman how valid it is to say that most people have a bent either for words or for numbers.

"You could certainly divide people into those two rough categories," she said, "but within those categories there are big differences in how people think. Last week in seventh grade we were doing an algebra problem about how much it would cost to take x number of kids to the movies. The movie tickets cost $3, it costs $28 to rent the bus, and there's $150 to spend. The algebraic sentence we were working with was $3x + 28 = 150$. I asked the students to talk about it—to describe what the sentence meant. Their perceptions of what it meant differed a great deal. One child clearly saw a number as the solution to the sentence; he was fixed on the answer. Another child saw what *I* was interested in—that it doesn't matter what x is, but that when you multiply it by 3 you can find out how much money you'll have to spend for *any* number of people if the tickets cost $3. I've never been all that interested in the right answer; I don't really care how many people I can take to the movies. I want students to see mathematics as a way of asking questions."

I was reminded of the philosophy professor at Gustavus Adolphus College who told me that many of his best student papers had been failures—papers in which the student explained why he couldn't get where he wanted to go. I asked Mrs. Countryman if it was possible to be a good math student and still not get the right answer.

"It certainly is—up to a point," she said. "Today the advanced placement exam in calculus has 50 percent multiple-choice questions and 50 percent 'free-response essays,' where the examiners give credit for the amount of information that's given instead of worrying about what *isn't* given. One of the things we keep telling the kids is: 'You can get credit, even if you don't know what the area under the figure is, if you give evidence that you know how to do it: how to set the problem up and what the boundaries are.' In advanced calculus papers I've seen kids write, 'I don't know how to evaluate this integral, but if I *could* evaluate it I'd get the area.' I think that's fascinating."

Listening to these examples, I saw that many of my beliefs about writing and learning also apply to mathematics: that we write to discover what we know and don't know; that we write more comfortably if we go exploring, free of the fear of not being on the "right" road to the right destination, and that we learn more if we feel that the work has a purpose. Motivation is as important in mathematics writing as in every other kind of writing. I asked Joan Countryman how she keeps alive the awareness that math is closely related to life.

"There's no dearth of topics for math papers," she said, "but often students seem to be just meeting an assignment instead of pursuing a genuine interest of theirs. I'm always looking for a connection between mathematics and social questions. Recently in my twelfth-grade calculus class the lesson was on exponential functions, and I wanted to find an example of exponential growth that would make sense to the kids. One method that we have in math is to construct a mathematical model that uses exponential functions. It enables you to get at all kinds of world problems."

The model that she found for her class began like this:

Let's suppose that the population of the world today is 4.7 billion and is growing at the rate of 1.64% per year, which is very close to the actual figures. This doesn't seem like much of a growth rate, but let's see what the implications are.

Then it posed a series of numerical questions that would lead the student to some disturbing answers. Then, switching gears, it offered another example of exponential growth:

> Bacteria grow by cell division. One cell divides to produce two. Two produce four, four produce eight, and so on. Suppose that we start with one bacterium in a jar, that each will divide once each minute, and that the jar is full at 12:00 noon. When is it half full?

Then it posed another set of numerical questions, one of which told the students to suppose that three more bottles were discovered and to calculate how long it would take to fill them also.

From this model Joan Countryman asked her students to write a paper that would draw an analogy between population growth and bacterial growth and to say whether they could see a "simple" solution to the problem of population growth. One of the essays she got back was this one by seventeen-year-old Hasan Mooney:

> The examples of bacteria growth and world population are analogous in that both increase the numbers exponentially. This seems obvious but actually is intimidating when you consider that although the rate of increase is constant, the amount of increase every year (or minute) gets larger and larger without bound.
>
> Well, this is not entirely true. The bacteria example was simply a mathematical model, and for that it was O.K. to assume that growth could continue infinitely. That idea helped to demonstrate how quickly the bacteria would fill up three extra bottles.
>
> There are a couple of problems in comparing this to the world population. First, we have no three extra bottles (extra planets?) to drop people into. Also, after a time it will become

impossible for the growth rate to continue as it is, for the same reason: that there is a limited amount of space and that extra crowding will lead to disease, food shortage, war, etc.

I don't believe there is a simple solution to the population problem. Certainly it would be very useful to reduce the growth rate through mass education or birth control. But people will always have kids. It is also important to learn to conserve and maximize the resources we have.

"A problem like that one has many advantages," Joan Countryman said. "First, for a kid who likes to write, there's a lot to say. The math isn't too hard, and it also suggests certain obvious techniques for producing an answer: for example, choosing a population of a certain size and making certain assumptions about childbearing age. A similar problem that I gave my class was this: Suppose every family in China was allowed to have children until they had a son. What effect would that have on population growth, and would it change the proportion of males and females in the country? The result was very surprising. The students not only wrote their way through the mathematics of exponential growth; they raised many interesting side issues of economics and agriculture and social structure. One girl pointed out that no Chinese boy would ever have a brother."

One by-product of these essays is the reminder that mathematical models are fallible; human nature will always have the last word. "Models enable us as citizens to ask, 'Do we have control over the problem?'" Mrs. Countryman said. "In the case of the bacteria in the bottle, the model does what it's supposed to do: It produces an answer. But the point that Hasan makes in his paper is that you have to be careful that your model relates to the world, because very often it leaves out significant problems. I don't think these larger issues would have occurred to students who only used mathematical methods to get their answer. Writing is what forced them to think through both the math and its relationship to their own lives."

*

Physiological note: I had been sitting in Joan Countryman's living room for two hours talking about mathematics. My pulse was steady, the hand that held my note-taking pencil didn't shake and wasn't even clammy. Where was that old math anxiety? I hadn't been at any loss for questions; they came to me naturally. Like the process of writing, the process of asking questions had been a form of learning, raising further questions and telling me what I wanted to know next. I was genuinely curious. It never occurred to me that this was a subject I wasn't supposed to be any good at. What did occur to me was that mathematics was not some arcane system of numbers; it was a language, a way of putting thoughts together. I might never master the language—my checkbook might still go unbalanced—but at least I had begun to glimpse what the language was trying to say and how it could help people to understand the world around them.

By extension, I thought, this must also be true of engineering, chemistry, biology and all the other special languages that have been invented to express special ideas. They can be at least broadly apprehended. What keeps us from trying is fear; the engineer is as frightened of my language (writing) as I am of his. Scared away by the probable difficulty of learning the language, we never get to its literature—the purpose it was created for.

I asked Joan Countryman whether the new technology of computers could knock this barrier down.

"That's one of the things that got me thinking about writing," she said. "In the face of so much new technology, math teachers are starting to have to rethink what they do. For instance, all that algebra we used to spend weeks teaching—factoring and quadratic equations—is available today on a little piece of software that a school can buy for less than fifty dollars. I don't think you can make a case for teaching quadratic equations anymore; 95 percent of the general population can't solve them anyway. Instead you can give your class a problem that requires a quadratic equation and let the machine solve the equation. That liberates you to think about what makes the problem interesting and what its ramifications are. In the past, kids spent all their time figuring out how to do the equation.

"I made this point at a conference of math teachers a few years ago. I said that to take advantage of the computer you could have kids do some writing about the problems they're trying to solve. In fact, you could have them write their own problems and make up their own questions. That's totally new to students. I was surprised by the teachers' response. There were teachers at the conference from states like Nebraska and Rhode Island and Washington, which had a mandate from the board of education to do writing across the curriculum, and the math teachers were resisting it because they didn't know what the writing might be. So they said, 'Tell us more—what are you doing?' I went home and wrote a paper called 'Writing to Learn Mathematics,' which is just a set of ideas about the kind of things you can do, and that led to all these workshops."

I was struck by the fact that for students to make up their own problems was something "totally new." Only then did it come back to me from my boyhood that the math teacher not only has custody of all the right answers; the teacher (or his surrogate, the textbook) also provides all the questions. I thought of the countless hours I had spent in math classes determining how long it took those three musketeers of math pedagogy, A, B and C, rowing at different speeds, to reach a certain bend in the river. No suspense about the outcome relieved the monotony of those races, for the three rowers were as foreordained as figures in a morality play to finish in the same order. It was a matter of character. A was strong and handsome, honest and decent, patriotic and God-fearing; B was plucky but flawed, fated to catch his oar on a rock just when victory seemed possible; and C was the amiable bumbler who is every one of us, capsizing in the stream. I always hoped for an upset—for C to redeem the best dreams of life's losers, or at least for B to redeem the best dreams of life's runners-up. It was not to be; in algebra textbooks, life's races were rigged.

I explained to Joan Countryman that my conception of mathematics was largely rooted in the lives and fortunes of A, B and C. "Those problems," she said, "were the sole effort that textbooks made to establish a connection between math and the world. If your only notion of a math problem is those questions about A, B and C, or about those two trains going in opposite directions, that's a very limited notion of the kinds of things that mathematics does. But if you encourage students to write their *own* questions, there's no limit to where they can go."

One place they can go is into other disciplines, I suggested to Joan Countryman. "Obviously one of the things you're after is to break down the compartments between different subjects."

"I try to do that a lot," she said. "The tradition is that there should be a connection between math and what we call science. Actually, in most schools, math and science teachers don't have anything to do with each other. But in many fields there's a natural crossover. Philosophy, for instance. I co-teach an introductory course in philosophy with the woman who's head of our classics department. One thing I did was to read Euclid with the class, which normally isn't part of philosophy. It turned out that it was very useful to the kids because Euclid's style, which was to make propositions and derive theorems from them, was adopted by many later philosophers, like Spinoza. We've had a good time playing around with that, trying to figure out what some of the connections are. The kids were startled by it."

Another discipline with startling connections, I suggested, is history. From my days at the Book-of-the-Month Club I remembered when the first trickle of books of "new history" came along—books that use the new technology of numbers crunching to reconstruct the daily life of earlier eras. Two that took us by surprise with their popularity were *The Structures of Everyday Life* and *The Wheels of Commerce,* by the French historian Fernand Braudel, which were intimate accounts of how "ordinary" people lived and worked and made their money in Europe between the fifteenth and the eighteenth centuries. So strong was Braudel's influence that the Club was soon awash in histories—about medieval England, about czarist Russia, about revolutionary America—that were grounded in population figures, agricultural records and other quantitative data that scholars had never had before the advent of computers.

"It's a wonderful development," Joan Countryman agreed, "and because of it there's far more conversation now between history teachers and math teachers. I tell our history teachers that I'll put a history question on my test if they'll put a math question on their test. I'm teasing, of course."

It didn't strike me as a teasing notion. On the contrary, it was a unifying idea, one that summed up much of what we had been talking about all afternoon. "Wouldn't it be the same question?" I asked. "Wouldn't the history question on the math test be the same as the math question on the history test?" I had in mind some question like "How can we find out what people ate in eighteenth-century France?"

Mrs. Countryman said it could easily be the same question, and in both cases writing would be the tool for thinking about how to find the answer. That would make for unusually interesting mathematics, I thought, and also for interesting history. At least it would be more interesting than all those trips up—or was it down?—the river with A, B and C.

*

The next day I sat in on Joan Countryman's eleventh-grade precalculus class. The arriving students grabbed their notebooks from her desk and began to write in them intently. "This year I got braver," she explained to me, "and decided to have everybody just do free writing at the beginning of every class. 'Check your editor at the door,' I told them. 'You can write about anything as long as you're willing to have me see what it is.' What they write doesn't have to be about math, but half the time it is: 'Why does this formula function? What does this pattern of numbers mean?' Or it might be about one of their other subjects: 'Here's a physics experiment I tried that didn't come out right.' They seem to want to know what's going on inside their heads—what their learning styles are—and that's something I'm eager for them to know.

"I also talk with them individually about what they've written. One point I make is that if you grow up to be a middle-aged engineer you're going to need to write, and this is one way to make yourself comfortable with it. If only for that reason, keeping these notebooks is helpful. But it also turns out to do other things: it's a way of clearing the palate. Kids come into the classroom with all this other stuff in their heads. If they write it down for ten minutes they become much more available for whatever it is we want to do in the class. One of my colleagues worries that if she does this she'll get less teaching done because every class will be ten minutes shorter, but it doesn't seem to work out that way."

When free writing ended, math began. Mrs. Countryman drew a triangle on the blackboard and told the class she wanted them to determine the size of its three angles. But she gave them none of the information they would need—for instance, the length of the sides.

"I want you to write how you might go about solving this problem when you do get more information from me," she said. The students wrote for about five minutes. They looked like writers—they were thinking hard and laboriously putting sentences on paper and crossing out sentences that obviously didn't express what they were thinking, perhaps because their thinking kept changing as they wrote and discovered what they really thought. They even sounded like writers; I heard the scratching out of words that is the obbligato of a writer's life.

After that some of them were asked to read what they had written. The papers were all brief journeys in logic: if I knew *this* I'd be able to find out *that;* what I need to determine is *a,* so the best method to use is probably *x* and *y.* Writing and thinking and learning had merged into one process. The class was off to a good start, and when it got down to actual mathematics—when the students were given the length of the sides and began to do some calculating—they were working from a common understanding of how the problem should be approached. They threw numbers and suppositions and probabilities into the room until they got the first of the three angles, and the rest was easy.

Joan Countryman's part in all this had been to coax scraps of information out of the students until the pieces formed themselves into the right answer. I never felt that she was the owner of that answer. I almost had the feeling that she didn't know it herself; the answer was just there waiting to be found by all of them. What I did feel was that I was watching a very good teacher.

Earlier I had asked her how she happened to be at Germantown Friends. She said it was a homecoming. "The town where I spent my early childhood didn't have good enough schools to satisfy my parents," she explained. "At just about that time Germantown Friends decided that it wanted to integrate, but they were somewhat fearful because they didn't know what would happen. We were a black family that the school felt it could take a chance on. I went to the school for ten years, beginning in third grade. After that I went to Sarah Lawrence, where I had a wonderful math professor named Ed Cogan, and when I became a math teacher myself it seemed natural to start where I had begun. I've been here ever since. In fact, my own children have also gone through the school—they're both through Yale now—so my being here is part of a circle."

Now I was in her classroom with still another generation of math students; the circle was by no means closed. Thinking about the enjoyment that the students had brought to the problem of the triangle, I asked Joan Countryman what difference it would have made if no writing had been done—if she had provided the length of the triangle's three sides and told the class to figure it out by straight trigonometry.

"Two or three kids with an aptitude for numbers would probably have come up with a fairly quick answer," she said, "but even they wouldn't have thought about what they were doing as thoroughly as they did when they wrote about how they would do it. And the rest of the kids wouldn't have been forced to think about it at all; they would have just waited for someone else to come up with the answer. Writing gets everybody involved."

I wondered how sanguine Joan Countryman was about converting other math teachers to her approach. Resistance to new teaching methods usually takes one of two forms: conservatism ("We've always done it our way") or inertia ("Your way is too much work").

"It's mostly inertia," she said. "At math conferences teachers ask how much time it's going to take to work with this kind of writing, and all of us who are doing it say it doesn't take as much time as you'd think, especially because we're not teaching writing; we're teaching mathematics. I do occasionally make corrections, or comments, or tell them how to spell Pythagoras; if you're going to write about geometry you ought to be able to spell the words that geometry mentions. But I'm not so concerned about that. And I'm not concerned about writing style at all. What happens is that you just come to celebrate those wonderful phrases and sentences that the kids write. The writing jumps out at you."

10. Man, Woman and Child

One of the jobs I most enjoyed during my years at the Book-of-the-Month Club was to run an annual series of six lectures—sponsored by the Club and held at the New York Public Library—in which writers talked about a particular aspect of the art and craft of writing. The talks were taped, and at the end of each series I edited the transcripts into a book.

The first series was on the craft of biography, and the biographers included Robert A. Caro, who was then well into his three-volume life of Lyndon Johnson, and David McCullough, then in mid-pursuit of people who had known his subject, Harry Truman, in Independence, Missouri. Another year the theme was religious writing, the writers being, among others, Mary Gordon, the Catholic novelist, and Allen Ginsberg, the Buddhist poet.

But the series that comes back to me now, as I recall literature that I've admired about the species called man, was on the craft of memoir. I'm a pushover for memoir; to me it's the most powerful of nonfiction forms because it goes to the deepest roots of personal experience. Unlike autobiography, which covers an entire life, the memoirist focuses on one period that was unusually vivid or that was framed by historical events—childhood, for instance, or war. Memoir is a window into a life, and in our lecture series writers as different as Russell Baker, Annie

Dillard, Alfred Kazin and Toni Morrison took us into corners of
their past that had a heightened degree of emotion.

Lewis Thomas, however, had a different journey in mind. Dr.
Thomas first served notice with *Lives of a Cell,* in 1974, that a
cell biologist can also be a lyrical writer. But I had chosen him
for the series because of a later book called *The Youngest Science,* which is a memoir—in fact, two memoirs. On one level
it's Dr. Thomas's story of his own life as a doctor, starting with
his boyhood when he accompanied his father, a general practi-
tioner, on his rounds. Medicine was then "a profoundly ignorant occupation," and his father carried only four medications
in his black bag because they were the only ones that were
known to do any good. On another level it's the story of the
coming of age of American medicine, starting with the wartime
discovery of antibiotics, which made doctors far less ignorant
and helpless. I hoped Lewis Thomas would tell us how he had
gone about writing that double narrative. His talk started like
this:

To begin personally, on a confessional note, I was at one
time, at my outset, a single cell. I have no memory of this stage
of my life, but I know it to be true because everybody says so.
There was a sort of half-life before that, literally half, when the
two half-endowed, haploid gametes, each carrying half my
chromosomes, were off on their own looking to bump into
each other and did so, by random chance, sheer luck, for
better or worse, richer or poorer, et cetera, and I got under
way.

I do not remember this, but I know that I began dividing.
I have probably never worked so hard, and never again with
such skill and certainty. At a certain stage, very young, a matter of hours of youth, I sorted myself out and became a system
of cells, each labeled for what it was to become—brain cells,
limbs, liver, the lot—all of them signaling to each other, calcu-

lating their territories, laying me out. At one stage I possessed an excellent kidney, good enough for any higher fish; then I thought better and destroyed it all at once, installing in its place a neater pair for living on land. I didn't plan on this when it was going on, but my cells, with a better memory, did.

Thinking back, I count myself lucky that I was not in charge at the time. If it had been left to me to do the mapping of my cells I would have got it wrong, dropped something, forgotten where to assemble my neural crest, confused it. Or I might have been stopped in my tracks, panicked by the massive deaths, billions of my embryonic cells being killed off systematically to make room for their more senior successors, death on a scale so vast that I can't think of it without wincing. By the time I was born, more of me had died than had survived. It is no wonder I can't remember; during that time I went through brain after brain for nine months, finally contriving the one model that could be human, equipped for language.

This was terrific stuff, but it caught me off guard—it had never occurred to me that a memoir could be prenatal. I was reassured, however, by the word "language"; Dr. Thomas would soon get himself born and his chronology would move forward. It didn't.

It is because of language that I am able now to think farther back into my lineage. By myself, I can only remember two parents, one grandmother and the family stories of Welshmen, back into the shadows when all the Welsh were kings, but no farther. From there on I must rely on reading the texts.

They instruct me that I go back to the first of my immediate line, the beginner, the earliest *Homo sapiens,* human all the way through, or not quite human if you measure humanness as I do by the property of language and *its* property, the consciousness of an indisputably singular, unique self. I'm not sure how far back that takes me, and no one has yet told me about this convincingly. When did my relations begin speaking?

Writing is easier to trace, having started not more than a few years back, maybe 10,000 years, not much more. Tracking speech requires guesswork. If we were slow learners, as slow as we seem to be in solving today's hard problems, my guess is that we didn't begin talking until sometime within the last 100,000 years, give or take 50,000. That's what's called a rough scientific guess. But no matter, it is an exceedingly short time ago, and I am embarrassed at the thought that so many of my ancestors, generations of them—all the way back to the very first ones a million-odd years ago—may have been speechless. I am modestly proud to have come from a family of toolmakers, bone scratchers, grave diggers, cave painters. Humans all. But it hurts to think of them as so literally dumb, living out their lives without metaphors, deprived of conversation, even small talk. I would prefer to have had them arrive fully endowed, talking their heads off, the moment evolution provided them with braincases large enough to contain words, so to speak. But it was not so, I must guess, and language came late.

By now it was dawning on me that this was no ordinary excursion into the past. It was the story of what it means to be human. Still, something in me continued to want Lewis Thomas to get to his own humanity: How did this twentieth-century descendant of toolmakers and bone scratchers learn to use so compellingly the language that all those generations of his forebears never possessed at all? To be human is to want a tidy conclusion. Dr. Thomas pressed on:

What sticks in my mind is another, unavoidable aspect of my genealogy, far beyond my memory, but remembered still, I suspect, by all my cells. It is a difficult and delicate fact to mention. To face it squarely, I come from a line that can be traced straight back, with some accuracy, into a near-infinity of years before my first humanoid ancestors turned up. I go back, and so do you, like it or not, to a single Ur-ancestor whose remains are on display in rocks dated approximately 3.5 thousand million years ago, born a billion or so years after the earth itself took shape and began cooling down. That first of the line, our n-granduncle, was unmistakably a bacterial cell.

I cannot get this out of my head. It has become the most important thing I know, the obligatory beginning of any memoir, the long-buried source of language. We derive from a lineage of bacteria, and a very long line at that. Never mind our embarrassed indignation when we were first told, last century, that we came from a family of apes and had chimps as near-cousins. That was relatively easy to accommodate, having at least the distant look of a set of relatives. But this new connection, already fixed by recent science beyond any hope of disowning the parentage, is something else again. At first the encounter must come as a kind of humiliation. Humble origins indeed.

Around here I finally told myself to relax and enjoy the trip, wherever it was going. Ask a cell biologist to talk about memoir and he won't be satisfied until he gets back to the original cell. Only once did the collection of cells known as Lewis Thomas enter his own narrative. "I do have a few memories," he said, "of studying to read and write, age four or five, I think, but I have no earlier recollection at all of learning speech. This surprises me. You'd think that the first word, the first triumphant finished sentence, would have been such a stunning landmark to remain fixed in memory forever, the biggest moment in life. But I have forgotten." His brief appearance over, Dr. Thomas plunged back into the abyss, taking us on a voyage of unimaginable length—nothing less than a memoir of life on earth. "We are all," he said, "in the same family—grasses, seagulls, fishes, fleas and voting citizens of the republic."

I've slightly bent the rules of this book by presenting a talk instead of a piece of writing. Obviously, however, this is a piece of writing—nobody could improvise such a graceful chain of sentences—and by now it has properly found its way into a book. But mainly I'm using it to make a point about unexpectedness. I had a preconceived notion of what Lewis Thomas was going to say. More presumptuously, I had a notion of what I wanted him to say. What he *did* say was vastly more exciting than anything I could have conceived of. I loved how thoroughly he smashed my pious expectations. Originality and surprise are the most refreshing elements in nonfiction writing. There's no "right" way to approach the subject of memoir, or the subject of man, or any other subject. A writer who comes at his discipline from an oblique angle is almost always more fun to travel with. Risk gives writing an edge.

*

Of the many disciplines that deal with the study of man, one that appeals to me is anthropology. I can trace the seeds of my interest to a night on Broadway in 1952. In those years journalistic duty required me to attend every opening, and so it happened that I found myself in the Fulton Theater waiting for a show called *Dancers of Bali* to begin. The troupe was from the Balinese village of Pliatan, and I had no idea what I was in for. Nowhere had my life or my education been touched by the culture of Southeast Asia.

The curtain went up and the gamelan orchestra on the stage struck a note that went through me like an electrical current. It was a tremendous CLANG! that reverberated through the theater. Then the gamelan began to play, and I was an instant convert. What wonderful combination of instruments was making this wonderful sound? I saw that about twenty-five Balinese men, sitting cross-legged on the stage, were striking an array of gongs, cymbals, drums and metallophones with a rhythmical intricacy that was like nothing I had ever heard. No visible signal passed among them, but the precision was absolute, and although the Balinese scale contained only five notes, it seemed to keep renewing itself and to have unending variety because the percussion instruments were so alive.

Next the actors began to appear, some of them costumed as witches and dragons, performing Balinese dances that enacted the island's legends and religious beliefs, including the potent *kris* dance, in which the men went into a deep and ominous trance. The beauty and intensity of the dancers was joined with the beauty and intensity of the music—a perfect fusion of art and ritual. Yet we were told that this troupe, though probably Bali's best, was not untypical of what might be found in almost any Balinese village. That would be worth testing, I thought, and on my next summer vacation I took off for Indonesia.

First I went to Jogjakarta, in central Java, to see the ancient shadow plays of the Javanese court, which also had a gamelan accompaniment. Those stylized dramas put me in the mood for Bali, and when I got there I made my way up into the hills to the village of Pliatan. The musicians and dancers who had conquered Broadway had long since come home and were back at their everyday jobs in the rice fields. That's how I found out that the Balinese have almost no concept of "art." What I had assumed was their art turned out to be organic to their life. Night after night, standing in the dirt temple courtyard in Pliatan, Ubud and other villages, I watched the same dances that I had seen on Broadway, performed by men and women who during the day had been working. Art, life and religion were intertwined. Children and chickens were everywhere. Mothers holding their babies stood in a circle around the dancers; the delicate movements of the dancers and the clinking sounds of the gamelan got absorbed almost from birth.

That was my first view of a unified culture, and I remember how resentful I felt that my own culture didn't have such an enviable wholeness. I thought of how American schools treat the arts as frills—a detour off the main road of education—and how religion is something that's done on Sunday morning. I wondered how often in my earlier travels I had patronized as "quaint" some entirely sensible custom of another country. Bali was the beginning of my treatment—still far from over—for the disease of ethnocentricity. Since then I've been impatient with travel pieces that rhapsodize over quaint Dutch farmers wearing wooden shoes or picturesque muezzins calling the Muslim faithful to prayer. We have plenty of quaint customs of our own; recently I saw a Japanese tourist taking a snapshot of a Park Avenue matron who was scooping the droppings of her poodle into a bag, as required by our New York "leash law."

Hence my admiration for the writing of anthropologists, who bring to each culture an austere objectivity, free of prior judgment, unlike sociologists, who come bearing certitudes about how everybody should behave. Anthropologists also tend, unlike sociologists, to write well; they disdain slippery language and easy escapes. You can open Margaret Mead's books to any page and find yourself in the company of a careful observer describing an alien society with rigorous clarity, detail and respect. Here's a page from her *Growing Up in New Guinea:*

In Manus there is neither heaven nor hell; there are simply two levels of existence. On one level live the mortals, all of whose acts, each of whose words, are known to the spirits, provided the spirit is present and paying attention. The spirit is not conceived as omniscient. He, like a living man, can only see and hear within the range of his senses. A spirit will disclaim knowledge of what went on in a house during his absence. Spirits are invisible, only rarely are they seen by mortals, but they occasionally make their presence manifest by whistling in the night. They are more powerful than mortals, being less dependent upon time and space and having the power to translate material objects into their own sphere of invisibility.

They act upon mortals by extracting bits of the soul stuff. If all of a mortal's soul stuff is taken by a spirit or spirits the mortal will die. Spirits can also hide things, steal things, throw stones, and otherwise manipulate the material world in a capricious, unaccountable fashion. This, however, they very seldom do. In spite of their greater powers they are conceived very humanly. So a man will beseech his spirit to drive an expected school of fish into a particular lagoon. He will not ask his spirit to multiply the fish, only to herd them. The chief duties of a spirit are to prosper the fishing of his wards and to preserve their lives and limbs against the machinations of hostile spirits.

It is the spirits' privilege to demand in return the exercise of certain restraints and virtues. In the first place, the living must commit no sex offenses which interfere with the Manus social order (i.e.: a spirit will not object to an intrigue with a woman of another tribe). This is a rigorous prohibition; light words, chance physical contacts, evil plans, careless jests, non-observance of the proper avoidance reactions toward relatives-in-law, all these may bring down the spirits' righteous wrath, either upon the sinner or upon some one of his relatives—perhaps pushing a decrepit old man from his lingering bed into death, perhaps afflicting a newborn baby with the colic.

Additionally, the spirits abhor economic laxity of any sort: failure to pay debts, careless manipulation of family properties, economic procrastination, and unfair allotment of funds among the needs of several relatives, as when a man uses all the wealth which comes into the family to make spectacular payments for his wife and fails to make betrothal payments for his younger brothers. Insubordination within a family, quar-

rels between in-laws also stir their wrath. And bad housing
annoys the critical spirits, who object to presiding over unsafe
floors, sagging piles, and leaky thatch.

What an amazing wealth of information Margaret Mead
packs into that one passage. She is truly a recording angel. Her
scholarly pleasure is to get it right and get it down for the use
of other scholars.

Beneath all such research, of course, is a staggering amount
of work on the part of the anthropologist to become accepted
by the people of the community as an observer in their midst,
to learn their language, and to record and transcribe endless
notes—an effort measured in years, not months. Even a nonfiction writer who conducts extensive interviews for an article or
a book has no conception of such labor. The reader can only
guess at the magnitude of the feat from the meticulous detail
of the results.

What often does get described, however, is the process of
acceptance by the local culture—the anthropologist walking
the thin line of approval. An engaging example is Clifford
Geertz's preamble to his famous essay "Deep Play: Notes on the
Balinese Cockfight."

That Geertz was drawn to Bali during his illustrious career is
hardly a coincidence; no piece of land on the face of the earth
has been so anthropologized. The music and dance that cap-
tivated me are only two of many strands in a web of identifying
traits found nowhere else. Equally distinctive to Bali, Geertz
points out, are its mythology, art, ritual, social organization,
patterns of child rearing, forms of law and even styles of trance.
But the cockfight, he says, "has barely been noticed, although
as a popular obsession of consuming power it is at least as important a revelation of what being Balinese 'is really like' as these
more celebrated phenomena. As much of America surfaces in

a ball park, on a golf links, at a race track, or around a poker table, much of Bali surfaces in a cock ring."

This is how Geertz's classic study of that popular obsession got off to its highly unscientific start:

Early in April of 1958, my wife and I arrived, malarial and diffident, in a Balinese village we intended, as anthropologists, to study. A small place, about five hundred people, and relatively remote, it was its own world. We were intruders, professional ones, and the villagers dealt with us as Balinese seem always to deal with people not part of their life who yet press themselves upon them: as though we were not there. For them, and to a degree for ourselves, we were nonpersons, specters, invisible men. . . .

When you first meet a Balinese, he seems virtually not to relate to you at all; he is, in the term Gregory Bateson and Margaret Mead made famous, "away." Then—in a day, a week, a month (with some people the magic moment never comes)—he decides, for reasons I have never quite been able to fathom, that you *are* real, and then he becomes a warm, gay, sensitive, sympathetic, though, being Balinese, always precisely controlled, person. You have crossed, somehow, some moral or metaphysical shadow line. Though you are not exactly taken as a Balinese (one has to be born to that), you are at least regarded as a human being rather than a cloud or a gust of wind. The whole complexion of your relationship changes to, in the majority of cases, a gentle, almost affectionate one—a low-keyed, rather playful, rather mannered, rather bemused geniality.

Geertz explains that he and his wife were still "very much in the gust-of-wind stage" when a large cockfight was held to raise money for a new school. Though such fights were illegal, the villagers thought that because their cause was worthy and "the necessary bribes had been paid" they could safely hold the fight in a relatively public part of the village.

They were wrong. In the midst of the third match, with hundreds of people, including, still transparent, myself and my wife, fused into a single body around the ring, a super-organism in the literal sense, a truck full of policemen armed with machine guns roared up. Amid great screeching cries of "pulisi! pulisi!" from the crowd, the policemen jumped out, and, springing into the center of the ring, began to swing their guns around like gangsters in a motion picture, though not going so far as actually to fire them. The superorganism came instantly apart as its components scattered in all directions. People raced down the road, disappeared headfirst over walls, scrambled under platforms, folded themselves behind wicker screens, scuttled up coconut trees. Cocks armed with steel spurs sharp enough to cut off a finger or run a hole through a foot were running wildly around. Everything was dust and panic.

Even in the dust and panic the anthropologist had his eyes open for the human details of flight. His paragraph has the comic exactitude of a Keystone Cops movie script.

On the established anthropological principle, "When in Rome," my wife and I decided, only slightly less instantane-ously than everyone else, that the thing to do was run too. We ran down the main village street, northward, away from where we were living, for we were on that side of the ring. About halfway down another fugitive ducked suddenly into a compound—his own, it turned out—and we, seeing nothing ahead of us but rice fields, open country, and a very high volcano, followed him. As the three of us came tumbling into the courtyard, his wife, who had apparently been through this sort of thing before, whipped out a table, a tablecloth, three chairs, and three cups of tea, and we all, without any explicit communication whatsoever, sat down, commenced to sip tea, and sought to compose ourselves.

Still no letup. Mack Sennett couldn't have contrived a more enjoyable chase.

A few moments later, one of the policemen marched importantly into the yard, looking for the village chief. (The chief had not only been at the fight, he had arranged it. When the truck drove up he ran to the river, stripped off his sarong, and plunged in so he could say, when at length they found him sitting there pouring water over his head, that he had been away bathing when the whole affair had occurred and was ignorant of it. They did not believe him and fined him three hundred rupiah, which the village raised collectively.) Seeing me and my wife, "White Men," there in the yard, the policeman performed a classic double take. When he found his voice again he asked, approximately, what in the devil did we think we were doing there. Our host of five minutes leaped instantly to our defense, producing an impassioned description of who and what we were, so detailed and so accurate that it was my turn, having barely communicated with a living human being save my landlord and the village chief for more than a week, to be astonished. We had a perfect right to be there, he said. We were American professors; the government had cleared us; we were there to study culture; we were going to write a book to tell Americans about Bali. And we had all been there drinking tea and talking about cultural matters all afternoon and did not know anything about any cockfight. Moreover, we had not seen the village chief all day; he must have gone to town. The policeman retreated in rather total disarray. And, after a decent interval, bewildered but relieved to have survived and stayed out of jail, so did we.

The paragraph has a double-take quality of its own. Beneath a veneer of knockabout farce Geertz has given us a striking fact about the Balinese character, as impressive as any that he will discover by more orthodox methods during the remainder of his stay. Here's the payoff:

> The next morning the village was a completely different world for us. Not only were we no longer invisible, we were suddenly the center of all attention, the object of a great outpouring of warmth, interest, and, most especially, amusement. Everyone in the village knew we had fled like everyone else. They asked us about it again and again (I must have told the story, small detail by small detail, fifty times by the end of the day), gently, affectionately, but quite insistently teasing us: "Why didn't you just stand there and tell the police who you were?" "Why didn't you just say you were only watching and not betting?" "Were you really afraid of those little guns?" As always, kinesthetically minded and, even when fleeing for their lives, the world's most poised people, they gleefully mimicked, also over and over again, our graceless style of running and what they claimed were our panic-stricken facial expressions. But above all, everyone was extremely pleased and even more surprised that we had not simply "pulled out our papers" (they knew about those too) and asserted our Distinguished Visitor status, but had instead demonstrated our solidarity with what were now our co-villagers. (What we had actually demonstrated was our cowardice, but there is fellowship in that too.)
>
> In Bali, to be teased is to be accepted. It was the turning point so far as our relationship to the community was concerned, and we were quite literally "in." The whole village opened up to us, probably more than it ever would have otherwise, and certainly very much faster. Getting caught, or almost caught, in a vice raid is perhaps not a very generalizable recipe for achieving that mysterious necessity of anthropologi-

cal field work, rapport, but for me it worked very well. It led
to a sudden and unusually complete acceptance into a society
extremely difficult for outsiders to penetrate. It gave me the
kind of immediate, inside-view grasp of an aspect of "peasant
mentality" that anthropologists not fortunate enough to flee
headlong with their subjects from armed authorities normally
do not get. And, perhaps most important of all, for the other
things might have come in other ways, it put me very quickly
on to a combination emotional explosion, status war, and philosophical drama of central significance to the society whose
inner nature I desired to understand. By the time I left I had
spent about as much time looking into cockfights as into witch-
craft, irrigation, caste, or marriage.

In all of Geertz's essays I feel that he thinks of himself as a
writer. He is personal and spontaneous—having a good time
and writing above all for himself. Such humanity is so rare in the
prose of academics that it glitters when it appears, especially
because, as in this case, Professor Geertz has abdicated none of
his professional stature by writing in clear, robust English. On
the contrary, through his writing he has become not only a giant
of his own discipline, but an intellectual prophet to scholars in
other fields. A recent article about Princeton's "hot history department" in the *New York Times Magazine,* for instance,
noted his impact on a whole generation of historians.

"In the early 1970s," the article said, "it was not only at
Princeton that historians were beginning to read Geertz. In
universities around the country, graduate students and some of
their teachers could be heard wondering about how to 'make
use of the insights of anthropology,' and if there was a single text
that best conveyed those insights it was Geertz's essay, 'Deep
Play: Notes on the Balinese Cockfight.' " What Geertz did, as
one Princeton historian put it, was to "provide what he calls

local knowledge, a way of finding deep human meaning in small sets of relationships, creating a significance which didn't rely on transcendental expectations about change."

I wish more academics could present the fruits of their considerable knowledge and research in writing as broadly accessible as Geertz's books are, or as Lewis Thomas's books are. But I'm not waiting for that millennium. It's a fact of the publishing industry that at least 90 percent of the manuscripts that academics submit for general publication are too poorly written to be considered. Their style is one that has been decreed by other academics—gatekeepers of the lodge—as the passport to a Ph.D., to tenure and to the approval of their peers. It's a language squeezed dry of human juices—a Sargasso Sea of passive verbs, long and generalized nouns, pompous locutions and unnecessary jargon. "I can't help it—I've got to play by the rules," the perpetrators explain when they ask why they can't get a certain book or article published and are told the horrid truth. I find it hard to sympathize. Other people's rules are shackles on the mind. Timidity never produced a good piece of writing.

*

If the proper study of mankind is man, as Alexander Pope so self-evidently reminded us, one of the vital roles an anthropologist can play is to tell us who we are and what makes every race peculiarly different. One stimulating example is a book by the anthropologist Edward T. Hall, called *The Hidden Dimension,* that dimension being the "bubble" of personal space that surrounds every man, woman and child. How we feel about that bubble is how we define ourselves, Professor Hall says, pointing out that many well-meant works of architecture and city planning have come to grief over their failure to recognize this inexorable law of biology.

"Architects," Hall writes, "are traditionally preoccupied with the visual patterns of structures—what one sees. They are almost totally unaware of the fact that people carry around with them internalizations of fixed-feature space learned early in life." Man, he says, like other members of the animal kingdom, "is first, last and always a prisoner of his biological organism. No matter how hard he tries, it is impossible for him to divest himself of his own culture, for it has penetrated to the roots of his nervous system and determines how he perceives the world."

Thinking about that nervous system, Hall considers the fact that after two thousand years of contact, Westerners and Arabs still don't understand each other. Each is discomfited by the other's "sensory world." Why do Americans in the Middle East, for instance, feel so claustrophobic when they encounter Arabs in public places? Hall recalls how he stumbled on the answer:

> Pushing and shoving in public places is characteristic of Middle Eastern culture. Yet it is not entirely what Americans think it is (being pushy and rude) but stems from a different set of assumptions concerning not only the relations between people but how one experiences the body as well. . . . After repeated unsuccessful attempts to gain insight into the cognitive world of the Arab on this particular point, I filed it away as a question that only time would answer. When the answer came, it was because of a seemingly inconsequential annoyance.

The last sentence piques our curiosity. We absolutely must continue. Professor Hall maintains contact with the reader as biological organism, one that craves a story.

> While waiting for a friend in a Washington, D.C., hotel lobby and wanting to be both visible and alone, I had seated myself in a solitary chair outside the normal stream of traffic. In such a setting most Americans follow a rule, which is all the

more binding because we seldom think about it, that can be stated as follows: as soon as a person stops or is seated in a public place, there balloons around him a small sphere of privacy which is considered inviolate. The size of the sphere varies with the degree of crowding, the age, sex, and the importance of the person, as well as the general surroundings. Anyone who enters this zone and stays there is intruding. In fact, a stranger who intrudes, even for a specific purpose, acknowledges the fact that he has intruded by beginning his request with, "Pardon me, but can you tell me . . . ?"

As I waited in the deserted lobby, a stranger walked up to where I was sitting and stood close enough so that not only could I easily touch him but I could even hear him breathing. In addition, the dark mass of his body filled the peripheral field of vision on my left side. If the lobby had been crowded with people, I would have understood his behavior, but in an empty lobby his presence made me exceedingly uncomfortable. Feeling annoyed by this intrusion, I moved my body in such a way as to communicate annoyance. Strangely enough, instead of moving away, my actions seemed only to encourage him, because he moved closer.

By now we are caught up in the anthropologist's sensory gavotte. He has put us into his own chair, one that we realize we have often occupied—in the subway or some other public space—and always with mounting squeamishness.

In spite of the temptation to escape the annoyance, I put aside thoughts of abandoning my post, thinking, "To hell with it. Why should I move? I was here first and I'm not going to let this fellow drive me out even if he is a boor." Fortunately, a group of people soon arrived whom my tormentor immediately joined. Their mannerisms explained his behavior, for I knew from both speech and gestures that they were Arabs. I had not been able to make this crucial identification by looking at my subject when he was alone because he wasn't talking and he was wearing American clothes.

In describing the scene later to an Arab colleague, two contrasting patterns emerged. My concept and my feelings about my own circle of privacy in a "public" place immediately struck my Arab friend as strange and puzzling. He said, "After all, it's a public place, isn't it?" Pursuing this line of inquiry, I found that in Arab thought I had no rights whatsoever by virtue of occupying a given spot; neither my place nor my body was inviolate. For the Arab, there is no such thing as an intrusion in public. Public means public.

With this insight, a great range of Arab behavior that had been puzzling, annoying, and sometimes even frightening began to make sense. I learned, for example, that if A is standing on a street corner and B wants his spot, B is within his rights if he does what he can to make A uncomfortable enough to move. In Beirut only the hardy sit in the last row in a movie theater, because there are usually standees who want seats and who push and shove and make such a nuisance that most people give up and leave. Seen in this light, the Arab who "intruded" on my space in the hotel lobby had apparently selected it for the very reasons I had: it was a good place to watch two doors and the elevator. My show of annoyance, instead of driving him away, had only encouraged him. He thought he was about to get me to move.

This chance encounter in a hotel lobby prompts Professor Hall to ask himself whether Arabs have wholly different assumptions about the human body and the rights that are associated with it. In answering his own question he gives us, as always, specific examples. We never think: I get the general point, but what *exactly* does he mean?

Certainly the Arab tendency to shove and push each other in public and to feel and pinch women in public conveyances would not be tolerated by Westerners. It appeared to me that Arabs must not have any concept of a private zone outside the body. This proved to be precisely the case.

In the Western world, the person is synonymous with an individual inside a skin. And in northern Europe generally, the skin and even the clothes may be inviolate. You need permission to touch either if you are a stranger. This rule applies in some parts of France, where the mere touching of another person during an argument used to be legally defined as assault. For the Arab the relation of the person in relation to the body is quite different. The person exists somewhere down inside the body. The ego is not completely hidden, however, because it can be reached very easily with an insult. It is protected from touch but not from words.

*

Of course it's not necessary to go outside the United States, or even outside your hometown, to find a culture idiosyncratic enough to be worth writing about. Any enclosed clan will give an anthropologist ample food for thought about society as a whole, and today much good writing in the discipline is minutely local.

Nor does the anthropologist have a monopoly on helpful truth; other disciplines yield other insights. I think instantly—inevitably—of Robert Coles, a doctor and a child psychiatrist by training but also a fine writer. Coles has taken children as his constituency and their survival under stress as his passionate concern. It's hard to imagine any chronicle of our times more important or more impressive than his *Children of Crisis*.

A born-and-bred New Englander, Coles was sent in 1958 as an air force physician to Mississippi, a region that he "cared little to know." But the South at that moment happened to be

poised on the edge of a traumatic decade, one whose civil rights
struggles would inflict harsh pressures on black children, and
when Coles's two-year service was over he found that the South
had become a place, as he later wrote, "whose continuing pull
on my mind and heart prevents me from staying away very
long." That pull fixed the course of his life and produced *Children of Crisis.*

The following passage is from his introduction to Volume I.
I've chosen it for several reasons. It's well and warmly written.
It's also a good example of writing about three subjects that I
wanted to include in this book—medicine, psychiatry and children. It's also a prime example of the writer as citizen. In a
society whose priorities flagrantly favor the privileged, Coles
refuses to doze off. "Something's wrong here," *Children of Crisis* keeps telling us, but never in a voice that's didactic or political. Clinical detail is Coles's truth; the evidence that he accumu-
lates with the tools of his discipline is corrosive enough.

Finally, it may be worth asking—since this is a book about
writing in different disciplines—exactly what a discipline is.
How loosely or narrowly should we think about these arbitrary
containers of knowledge? How usefully can scholars define the
boundaries of their scholarship? Here's Robert Coles explaining
how he applied his discipline to the writing of *Children of
Crisis:*

> What I am trying to do is describe certain lives; specifically,
> describe the way those lives have come to terms with the
> political and social changes that have taken place in a particu-
> lar region of this country. If the book concerns itself with
> adults as well as children, its title accurately reflects my chief
> professional interest—though obviously no one can study chil-
> dren too long without taking a look at the people who nurture
> them, teach them, and on occasion fail them terribly. . . .
>
> I am working under the assumption that there still is room—

maybe a corner here and there—for direct, sustained observation of individual human beings living in a significant and critical period of history. By direct observation I mean talking with people, listening to them, watching them—and being watched by them. By sustained observation I mean taking a long time: enough time to be confused, then absolutely certain and confident, then not so sure but a little more aware of why one or another conclusion seems the best that can be argued, or at least better than any other available.

There is another qualifying word to the kind of observation I have attempted. It has been clinical, in the twin sense that I am a clinician and that I was looking at how children (or their parents and teachers) managed under stress; that is, abnormal and dangerous circumstances. The people I met had discernible cause to feel nervous, to develop a variety of symptoms in both mind and body. Whether they did so, and if they did how and when they did—such questions are reasonably the doctor's; while the psychiatrist, at least in this century, traditionally wants to know who chooses which kind of danger, and for what reason, known or unknown.

Even as a writer Coles is a clinician; that last sentence analyzes in the briefest space how the primary concern of the doctor differs from the primary concern of the psychiatrist. Having stated it, Coles explains how his own work, though he is both a doctor and a psychiatrist, doesn't quite fall in either camp:

What doctors and psychiatrists usually do not do is work with people who have no particular reason, interest or desire to see them—perhaps quite the opposite inclination. Medical students and psychiatrists in training are taught to understand the ways of disease, and then to heal pragmatically the illnesses that so often fail to follow the descriptions textbooks give to them. As a result, little if any medical or psychiatric attention is directed toward asking what exactly makes for survival under stress, for endurance, for courage against grim odds; indeed, for plain good health in contrast, say, to bad health and perhaps even bad "mental health," whatever that is.

Who is the "ordinary man," if he exists, and what does the word "normal" mean, if anything? What makes for persistence and stability in ordinary people (not patients)? What really does bring about the mind's collapse? A threshold of suffering passed? A long-standing weakness finally exposed, or given a decisive chance to do its bad work? Should we in medicine consider the economic indices or environmental settings that are sometimes summoned in the abstract as "causes" of this problem, or "factors" in that? What does the child's mind make of the world—of politics, race and the facts of money? Why does one person make satisfied peace with the world, while another takes the world on and tries to change it in any number of ways?

These are lovely questions, beautifully phrased. Can they be answered? Coles tells us whose job it is to try:

Social scientists have the job, the very necessary job, of documenting exactly what "outside" world it is—the time, the place, the culture and the society—that a particular child finds at birth and learns about as he grows. The clinician has always been interested in what goes on "inside" others—he himself being part of *their* "outside," their world. Presumably he is as qualified as anyone to go back and forth, to see how the two worlds (outside, inside) connect, blend, engage—words and images fail to describe the continuity between man's thinking and the world's state of affairs. So, what I have tried to pursue is a method of study (the clinical) and what I have tried to do is locate my body and mind where certain *citizens* are up against difficult times, so that their lives, like those of the sick, may have something to teach the rest of us.

Coles concludes by explaining that the process of writing Volume I of *Children of Crisis* made him realize that his labors, far from being over on the last page, were just starting. His foreword should therefore be viewed, he says, as the introduction to a work in progress, not just to one book. He saw as he wrote Volume I that the problems he had found in the South were "shared in one way or another by many other Americans." To pursue that discovery would ultimately require four more volumes:

What I learned as I came to know one family after another was that individual families share problems, just as regions and nations do. Many of the children I observed in Southern cities have cousins whose parents are migrant farmers, or sharecroppers, or "mountain folk" from the Appalachian hills of Virginia, North Carolina or Tennessee. Then, there are the cousins—not only Negroes, either—"abroad," in Chicago, New York or on the West Coast. When I finished the main, everyday part of my work with Southern children attending desegregated schools, I moved my concern to some of those cousins. I started looking further into the lives of migrant children, tenant farm and mountain children, and eventually the children of Northern cities who must also face social isolation, segregation, desegregation—in brief, the dislocated, hard living that is still America's gift to some of its young, regardless of race or ancestry. In future volumes—there seems no end to crisis in this world—I hope to tell of them and have them speak their own thoughts.

11. Writing Physics and Chemistry

Albert Einstein gazes out at me from the cover of a small paperback book called *Relativity: The Special and the General Theory,* looking not at all scary—looking, in fact, like a benign uncle who is about to tell me a story. The blurb on the cover says: A CLEAR EXPLANATION THAT ANYONE CAN UNDERSTAND. Albert Einstein is going to explain the theory of relativity to me. To *me?* That's what it says.

I've wanted to get the book ever since two science professors at Gustavus Adolphus College mentioned that it was a model of clear linear writing. At first that surprised me; I hadn't expected Einstein's theory to be reducible to plain English. But on second thought it made sense. If clear writing is clear thinking, a mind clear enough to think of the theory of relativity would be likely to express itself simply and well. The burden was therefore on me. Could a lifelong science boob follow Einstein's train of thought?

The only way to find out was to find out. I opened the book, which Einstein wrote, incidentally, in 1916, and plunged in:

In your schooldays most of you who read this book made acquaintance with the noble building of Euclid's geometry, and you remember—perhaps with more respect than love—the magnificent structure, on the lofty staircase of which you were chased about for uncounted hours by conscientious teachers. By reason of your past experience, you would certainly regard everyone with disdain who should pronounce even the most out-of-the-way proposition of this science to be untrue. But perhaps this feeling of proud certainty would leave you immediately if someone were to ask you: "What, then, do you mean by the assertion that these propositions are true?" Let us proceed to give this question a little consideration.

I hesitate to call that a good "lead"—to cling to the lingo of journalism while scaling the higher slopes of theoretical science. But it is in fact a delightful lead. In one paragraph Einstein reminds us of one of the great temples in intellectual history—Euclid's geometry—but also raises some doubts about how solid its foundations are today.

In paragraph two he tells us more about Euclid's "noble building":

Geometry sets out from certain conceptions such as "plane," "point" and "straight line," with which we are able to associate more or less definite ideas, and from certain simple propositions (axioms) which, by virtue of these ideas, we are inclined to accept as "true." Then, on the basis of a logical process, the justification of which we feel ourselves compelled to admit, all remaining propositions are shown to follow from those axioms, *i.e.* they are proven. A proposition is then correct ("true") when it has been derived in the recognized manner from the axioms. The question of the "truth" of the individual geometric propositions is thus reduced to one of the "truth" of the axioms.

Now it has long been known that the last question is not only unanswerable by the methods of geometry, but that it is in itself entirely without meaning. We cannot ask whether it is true that only one straight line goes through two points. We can only say that Euclidean geometry deals with things called "straight lines," to each of which is ascribed the property of being uniquely determined by two points situated on it. The concept "true" does not tally with the assertions of pure geometry, because by the word "true" we are eventually in the habit of designating always the correspondence with a "real" object; geometry, however, is not concerned with the relation of the ideas involved in it to objects of experience, but only with the logical connection of these ideas within themselves.

Still so far so good. If I understand Einstein—always a possibility—he's saying that Euclid's geometry is an abstract exercise that falls short of being applicable to the real world.

It is not difficult to understand why, in spite of this, we feel constrained to call the propositions of geometry "true." Geometrical ideas correspond to more or less exact objects in nature, and these last are undoubtedly the exclusive cause of the genesis of those ideas. Geometry ought to refrain from such a course, in order to give to its structure the largest possible logical unity. The practice, for example, of seeing in a "distance" two marked positions on a relatively rigid body is something which is lodged deeply in our habit of thought. We are accustomed further to regard these points as being situated on a straight line, if their apparent positions can be made to coincide for observation with one eye, under suitable choice of our place of observation.

If, in pursuance of our habit of thought, we now supplement the proposition of Euclidean geometry by the single proposition that two points on a practically rigid body always correspond to the same distance (line-interval), independently of any changes in position to which we may subject the body, the propositions of Euclidean geometry then resolve themselves into propositions on the possible relative position of practically rigid bodies. Geometry which has been supplemented in this way is then to be treated as a branch of physics. We can now legitimately ask as to the "truth" of geometrical propositions interpreted in this way, since we are justified in asking whether these propositions are satisfied for those real things we have associated with the geometrical ideas. In less exact terms we can express this by saying that by the "truth" of a geometrical proposition in this sense we understand its validity for a construction with ruler and compasses.

Of course the conviction of the "truth" of geometrical propositions in this sense is founded exclusively on rather incomplete experience. For the present we shall assume the "truth" of the geometrical propositions, then at a later stage (in the general theory of relativity) we shall see that this "truth" is limited.

That's Chapter 1 in its entirety. If the style is slightly rotund, remember that it was written in 1916, in German, a language of some rotundity. But there's nothing circular about the reasoning; Einstein's sentences move as sequentially as his mind evidently did in considering the problem in the first place. We are left with the idea that classical geometry has limitations but that modern physics can transcend them.

Next Einstein gives us a brief chapter called "The System of Co-ordinates," knowing that we won't understand how physics has pushed beyond geometry unless we first understand geometry's working principle: that it enables us "to establish the distance between two points on a rigid body by means of measurements":

Every description of the scene of an event or of the position of an object in space is based on the specification of the point on a rigid body (body of reference) with which that event or object coincides. This applies not only to scientific description, but also to everyday life. If I analyze the place specification "Trafalgar Square, London," I arrive at the following result. The earth is the rigid body to which the specification of place refers; "Trafalgar Square, London" is a well-defined point to which a name has been assigned and with which the event coincides in space.

This primitive method of place specification deals only with places on the surface of rigid bodies and is dependent on the existence of points on this surface which are distinguishable from each other. But we can free ourselves from these limitations without altering the nature of our specification of position.

How can we do that? "It should be possible by means of numerical measures," Einstein tells us, "to make ourselves independent of the existence of marked positions (possessing names) on the rigid body of reference." This brings him, in Chapter 3, into physics—specifically, into the question of "how bodies change their position in space with 'time.'"

With the mention of time, Einstein's story quickens; even *I* know that the theory of relativity deals with how moving objects are perceived in relation to both their own motion and the motion of the person observing them. Here's how Einstein introduces the principle:

I stand at the window of a railway carriage which is traveling uniformly, and drop a stone on the embankment without throwing it. Then, disregarding the influence of the air resistance, I see the stone descend in a straight line. A pedestrian who observes the misdeed from the footpath notices that the stone falls to the ground in a parabolic curve. I now ask: Do the "positions" traversed by the stone lie "in reality" on a straight line or on a parabola? Moreover, what is meant here by motion "in space"? The answer is self-evident. In the first place we entirely shun the vague word "space," of which, we must honestly acknowledge, we cannot form the slightest conception, and we replace it by "motion relative to a practically rigid body of reference." The positions relative to the body of reference (railway carriage or embankment) have already been defined in the preceding section. If instead of "body of reference" we insert "system of mathematical co-ordinates," which is a useful idea for mathematical description, we are in a position to say: The stone traverses a straight line relative to a system of co-ordinates rigidly attached to the carriage, but relative to a system of co-ordinates rigidly attached to the ground (embankment) it describes a parabola. With the aid of this example it is clearly seen that there is no such thing as an independently existing trajectory (or "path-curve"), but only a trajectory relative to a particular body of reference.

That's important information about the trajectory of the stone. It's not, however, information enough. We still need one more piece:

In order to have a *complete* description of the motion, we must specify how the body alters its position with *time; i.e.* for every point on the trajectory it must be stated what time the body is situated there.

So we are off on Einstein's great journey, which is no less epochal than Darwin's, and though I don't pretend to understand the formulations that he presents in subsequent chapters, never having taken a course in physics, I think I understand the general nature of his achievement and the thinking that took him there. I understand them because the writing and the reasoning remain orderly throughout.

Along the way Einstein also demystifies himself, continuing

to talk to me as a teacher talks to a student, using the written language as a step-by-step method of instruction. He even pauses occasionally—still the kind uncle of the cover photograph—to coddle us over leaps he knows we don't want to make: "The non-mathematician is seized by a mysterious shuddering when he hears of 'four-dimensional' things, by a feeling not unlike that awakened by thoughts of the occult. And yet there is no more commonplace statement than that the world we live in is a four-dimensional space-time continuum."

Tearing myself away from Albert Einstein—a parting I never imagined would be sweet sorrow—I'll add a final plea to all scientists and science students: Go, and do thou likewise. Follow Einstein's example and Thoreau's advice ("Simplify! Simplify!"). Reduce your discipline—whatever it is—to a logical sequence of clearly thought sentences. You will thereby make it clear not only to other people but to yourself. You will find out whether you know your subject as well as you thought you did. If you don't, writing will show you where the holes are in your knowledge or your reasoning.

*

Such instructional uses are by no means the only literary ends that disciplines like physics and chemistry can aspire to. Every science has its unique romance, and a writer who can capture that romance enables the rest of us to glimpse what it is about the field that makes it exciting to those who love it. It's one of the best gifts that science writing can confer.

No book has so put me inside the head and heart of a chemist as *The Periodic Table,* by Primo Levi, an Italian chemist who survived Auschwitz and wrote three powerful books about that experience. *The Periodic Table,* which was published in this country several years ago to great acclaim (in a superb translation by Raymond Rosenthal), takes its title from the structure of its chapters, each of which is named for a chemical element that played a memorable role at some moment in Levi's life. (He died in 1987.) Chapter 1, for instance, called "Argon," begins like this:

> There are the so-called inert gases in the air we breathe. They bear curious Greek names of erudite derivation which mean "the New," "the Hidden," "the Inactive," and "the Alien." They are indeed so inert, so satisfied with their condition, that they do not interfere in any chemical reaction, do not combine with any other element, and for precisely this reason have gone undetected for centuries. As late as 1962 a diligent chemist after long and ingenious efforts succeeded in forcing the Alien (xenon) to combine fleetingly with extremely avid and lively fluorine, and the feat seemed so extraordinary that he was given a Nobel prize. They are also called the noble gases—and here there's room for discussion as to whether all noble gases are really inert and all inert gases are noble. And finally, they are also called rare gases, even though one of them, argon (the Inactive), is present in the air in the considerable proportion of 1 percent, that is, twenty or thirty times more abundant than carbon dioxide, without which there would not be a trace of life on this planet.

I don't know many books that begin with such intellectual gusto. The sentences, like Einstein's, just flow from point to point, pulling us along with their enjoyment of the story and the language. Words that we don't expect to meet in science writing—"satisfied," "avid," "lively," "noble"—refresh us with their humanity.

One of my favorite chapters, "Tin," recalls a period in the author's twenties when he and his equally destitute friend Emilio were doing chemical odd jobs at home to make ends meet.

There are friendly metals and hostile metals. Tin was a friend—not only because, for some months now, Emilio and I were living on it, transforming it into stannous oxide to sell to the manufacturers of mirrors, but also for other, more recondite reasons: because it marries with iron, transforming it into mild tin plate; because the Phoenicians traded in it and it is to this day extracted, refined, and shipped from fabulous and distant countries; because it forms an alloy with copper to give us bronze, the respectable material par excellence, notoriously perennial and well established; because it melts at a low temperature, almost like organic compounds, that is, almost like us; and finally, because of two unique properties with picturesque, hardly credible names, never seen or heard (that I know) by human eye or ear, yet faithfully handed down from generation to generation by all the textbooks—the "weeping" of tin and tin pest.

That paragraph is the sort of thing I had in mind when I said that every science has its romance. It gives me a sense of the affection that chemists presumably feel for the elements that constitute their universe, each one a friend with idiosyncrasies that are—in the manner of friends—both lovable and annoying. I'm glad to know this about chemists and I'm grateful to Primo Levi for giving me a window into their world. His story continues:

Emilio had managed to carve a lab out of his parents' apartment. . . . When they let him take over their bedroom they had not foreseen all the consequences. . . . Now the hallway was a storeroom jammed with demijohns full of concentrated hydrochloric acid, the kitchen stove (outside of mealtime) was used to concentrate the stannous chloride in beakers and six-liter Erlenmeyer flasks, and the entire apartment was invaded with our fumes. . . . Everywhere, on the terrace and in the apartment, was scattered an incredible amount of junk, so old and battered as to prove almost unrecognizable: only after a more attentive examination could you distinguish the professional objects from the domestic ones.

In the middle of the lab was a large ventilation hood of wood and glass, our pride and our only protection against death by gasing. It is not that hydrochloric acid is actually toxic: it is one of those frank enemies that come at you shouting from a distance, and from which it is therefore easy to protect yourself. It has such a penetrating odor that whoever can wastes no time in getting out of its way; and you cannot mistake it for anything else, because after having taken in one breath of it you expel from your nose two short plumes of white smoke, like the horses in Eisenstein's movies, and you feel your teeth turn sour in your mouth, as when you have bitten into a lemon. Despite our quite willing hood, acid fumes invaded all the rooms: the wallpaper changed color, the doorknobs and metal fixtures became dim and rough, and every so often a sinister thump made us jump: a nail had been corroded through and a picture, in some corner of the apartment, had crashed to the floor.

So we were dissolving tin in hydrochloric acid. Then the solution had to be concentrated to a particular specific weight and left to crystallize by cooling. The stannous chloride separated in small, pretty prisms, colorless and transparent. Since the crystallization was slow, it required many receptacles, and since hydrochloric acid corrodes all metals, these receptacles had to be glass or ceramic. In the period when there were many orders, we had to mobilize reserve receptacles, in which for that matter Emilio's house was rich: a soup tureen, an enameled iron pressure cooker, an Art Nouveau chandelier, and a chamber pot.

The morning after, the chloride is gathered and set to drain, and you must be very careful not to touch it with your hands or it saddles you with a truly disgusting smell. This salt, in itself, is odorless, but it reacts in some manner with the skin, perhaps reducing the keratin's disulfide bridges and giving off a persistent metallic stench that for several days announces to all that you are a chemist. It is aggressive but also delicate, like certain unpleasant sports opponents who whine when they lose: you can't force it, you have to let it dry out in the air in its own good time. If you try to warm it up, even in the mildest manner, for example, with a hair dryer or on the radiator, it loses its crystallization water, becomes opaque, and foolish customers no longer want it. Foolish because it would suit them fine: with less water there is more tin and therefore more of a yield; but that's how it is, the customer is always right, especially when he knows little chemistry, as is precisely the case with mirror manufacturers.

That's the literature of chemistry with a capital *L*, proof that in sensitive hands any scientific subject can be made to soar. Unfortunately, I have to get back to earth and back to basics. In fact, I should put up a sign: PEDAGOGY AHEAD.

*

The premise of this book, as its title says, is that writing is how we think our way into a discipline, organize our thoughts about it and generate new ideas. I've left the premise largely unspoken, not wishing to repeat the same obvious point—that Darwin, for instance, was helped to arrive at a coherent theory about the Amblyrhynchus cristatus by putting his observations on paper, or that Rachel Carson clarified her hunches about "the sunless sea" by writing her way down into "these deep, dark waters, with all their mysteries and unsolved problems." Only in the chapter called "Writing Mathematics" did I document the learning process with classroom examples.

I want to do that one more time, taking chemistry as my model. I've chosen it partly to humor my sense of symmetry:

This book originated with a phone call from a chemistry professor, and it opens with my heretical failure to learn the subject as a boy. But mainly I've chosen chemistry because it's typical of all the sciences that use numbers, signs and symbols as a language and therefore don't seem to lend themselves to writing.

Writing, however, is one of the most powerful tools that science education possesses; a student can reason his way with words toward the solution of a problem and his teacher can watch him do it, or not do it. Although the following examples come from chemistry, you can adapt them to physics, biology, engineering, psychology and every other discipline where laboratory experiment and observation are a big part of the learning process. Just change the terminology to fit your field.

How does someone write chemistry? Here are two explanations that I like, taken from *The Journal of Chemical Education*. Chemistry teachers are now beginning to insist on writing from their students, and these two women are obviously leaders of the trend.

The first professor, Estelle K. Meislich, of Bergen Community College, Paramus, New Jersey, begins her article by raising the most common bugaboo that science teachers worry about: "Is there some way of requiring good writing from students that will not diminish the science content?" The concern behind the question is twofold: that teaching writing will take time away from teaching chemistry, and that writing in the sciences is "not the same" as writing in the humanities.

Tackling the question, Professor Meislich writes: "Here is a method I have used successfully for the past eight years in courses for both chemistry majors and nonmajors. On every examination I ask at least one and often several questions that require a written response. Students are told that their answers must be written in 'acceptable' English for credit. If I decide that a scientifically correct response is poorly written, the student cannot get credit for the correct answer until it is rewritten in correct English.

"The student has one week to return the rewritten paper for credit. During this time students are encouraged to meet with a writing instructor for help in rewriting. (I send the writing instructor a copy of the examination with correctly written answers to prepare him or her for students' requests for help.) Of course incorrect answers, no matter how well written, cannot be rewritten for credit.

"A paper that requires a rewritten answer will have two grades. The first one is for the originally submitted examination. The second grade, shown in parentheses, is the one that the student will receive if an acceptable rewritten answer is returned on time. . . . Once students accept the fact that correct but poorly written answers are unacceptable, most of them write more carefully. Eventually very few of them have to rewrite at all. In this way, writing becomes an integral part of the course without diminishing the chemical content."

Professor Meislich lists four kinds of questions that she asks on exams in her general and organic chemistry course for chemistry majors and her introductory course for nonmajors. One is a multiple-choice question with a twist: No credit is given for the right answer unless it's accompanied by a correct explanation. Typical questions are:

1. Which substance has a higher boiling point, CH_3CH_2OH or CH_3OCH_3?
2. Which has a smaller ionization energy, Na or Cs?

In another kind of question she asks students to explain why a given statement is false. Two such statements are:

1. According to modern atomic theory, electrons travel around the nucleus in well-defined orbits.

2. As more accurate instruments are constructed, scientists will be able to measure simultaneously the exact location and momentum of an electron.

The third type of question requires students to devise an experiment. For example:

How can you decide experimentally which layer in a separatory funnel is organic and which is aqueous? Describe what you would do, what you would see, and what you would conclude.

The fourth type of question asks for a brief essay. A typical essay topic is:

Living systems are more complex than nonliving systems, yet life started and exists on this planet. Explain why the existence of life does not violate the second law of thermodynamics.

Summing up her principles of writing to learn, Professor Meislich says: "Multiple-choice questions are very popular ways of testing knowledge, especially in classes with large numbers of students. However, a more complete understanding is demonstrated by the ability to explain. From the written explanations we get a better idea of the depth of the students' understanding. We can also learn about their possible misconceptions. Thus, written communication becomes an integral part of the course in a very direct way, with rapid feedback and the opportunity to correct errors in a nonpunitive manner.

"The ability to write well is a skill that students should be prepared to use in all courses. That is why I do not accept poorly written English in my chemistry classes." Nor, I might add, does she accept it from herself.

The second professor, Naola VanOrden, of Sacramento City

College, in California, notes that the inability of science students to write is a loss both to them and to society. Because science students gradually lose their freshman writing skills, she says, "employers complain that science graduates are technically competent but can't communicate. They are able to make reams of calculations but they can't explain the purpose for, or the significance of, those calculations." The problem was addressed by a recent national meeting of the American Chemical Society, which concluded that it had to be solved by chemistry departments, not by English departments.

"To motivate chemistry students to practice writing skills," Professor VanOrden says, "we must convince them that chemical writing is important. Writing assignments must be more than the usual end-of-chapter questions, which can be answered by copying the appropriate sentences from the chapter. They must require a synthesis of the concept fragments taught in the chapter." Above all, those assignments should have reality. "Just as we find that chemical calculations are more meaningful to students if they are related to the real world, so are chemical writing assignments more valuable if they illustrate real-life problems."

Where can such vignettes be found? Professor VanOrden reports that after years of searching she hit upon a type of brief writing assignment that succeeds because her students consider it an important part of her course. "These assignments are always related to the text concepts being studied," she says, "and many of them are examples of practical applications of chemical concepts. Students must first solve a chemical problem; then they must explain, discuss or apply their results."

At first her students are less than delighted by this prospect. "They complain that the assignments require too much time," Professor VanOrden says, "and also that 'this is a chemistry class, not an English class.' But by the third or fourth assignment they realize that *how* they write really does matter. Since most of my students are very serious and competitive, their writing quickly improves and many of them become quite creative. Perhaps the best evaluation of all is that, near the end of the semester, students bring me questions for future writing assignments. They have caught some of the vision of what education is trying to accomplish."

What kind of assignment would provoke a "quite creative" response? Here's one of Professor VanOrden's:

> You are the manager of River City Pet Store. A customer is very distraught because the fish in her backyard fish pond are dying. When she brings you a sample of the water, you find out that the pH of the water is 8.2, but this species of fish lives best in water of 6.8. (1) Select a good buffer system for a fish pond. (2) Calculate the quantities of buffer components that should be added to the pond to maintain the pH at 6.8. (3) Write a letter to the customer telling her how to treat her fish pond. (Make sure the buffer chemicals do not kill the fish.)

One student's response, as described by Professor VanOrden, took this form: "She selected the dihydrogen phosphate–monohydrogen phosphate buffer system and calculated the mole ratio necessary for a buffer of pH 6.8. Then she calculated the quantity of buffer components necessary to maintain the pH of five gallons of the pond water constant at pH 6.8. Next the student 'prepared' a product containing enough buffer for 1000 gallons of pond water. Then she 'marketed' the product under the trade name 'Aqua-lock.' The letter she wrote to her customer is as follows:"

Dear Mrs. Frame:

The completed analysis of your pond water indicates that a pH adjustment is needed to provide an adequate environment for your fish. Fortunately, this problem can be easily corrected with one of our products, Aqua-lock, pH 6.8. Aqua-lock is available in one-gallon jugs for only $25.95. I recommend that 5.5 quarts of the product be used immediately on your pond and once a month thereafter. Periodic maintenance thereafter could be cut down if you measure your pH and add the product only when the pH changes. Accordingly, I also recommend that you purchase Wardleys' Jr. pH Kit (instructions included) for only $14.98.

River City is committed to customer service. If we can be of further help, please feel free to call on us at any time.

Sincerely,

Valerie Ayala, Manager

As for the fear that teaching writing will take time away from teaching chemistry, Professor VanOrden says she makes no effort to teach grammar but does note errors of construction—sentences, for instance, that are ambiguous or awkward. "Help is available in the English writing lab," she points out, "but until I began grading writing assignments my students didn't take the time to get help because they didn't consider writing to be important to chemistry. Many of them still need help with the mechanics of sentence construction. We hope to solve this problem by establishing a drop-in writing lab just for science students."

But what Professor VanOrden is ultimately after is something that goes well beyond grammar or syntax, and the two sentences in her article that I liked most were these:

"I believe that writing is an effective means of improving thinking skills because a person must mentally process ideas in order to write an explanation. Writing also improves self-esteem because mentally processed ideas then belong to the writer and not just to the teacher or the textbook author."

With the word "self-esteem" Professor VanOrden put her finger on one of the most painful elements in writing. I recalled what Professor Gover told me when I asked him why even the science faculty at Gustavus Adolphus College had so strongly supported a writing-across-the-curriculum program. "Those of us who teach science and other technical subjects," he said, "have always felt insecure about writing. We knew we could deal well with ideas, but somehow when it came to putting words on paper it never came out right, and we heard about it, usually from our English teacher."

Who of us doesn't recognize that lament in some form from our own school days? Being made to feel dumb is not conducive to learning.

I believe, however, that writers often conspire in their own insecurity. (By "writers" I also mean every student of high school age and older who writes a paper of any kind.) Teachers of writing are dismally aware of the inclination of writers to equate the worth of their writing with the worth of who they are. The equation goes: "You think this is a terrible paper, therefore you must think I'm a terrible person."

The thought is natural, perhaps almost inevitable: when we write we put some part of our self on paper for other people to judge. But finally that thought is a self-indulgence. Writers who think *they* are being criticized when only their writing is being criticized are beyond a teacher's reach. Writing can only be learned when a writer coldly separates himself from what he has written and looks at it with the objectivity of a plumber examining a newly piped bathroom to see if he got all the joints tight.

Do I hear a gasp? How dare I compare writing to plumbing? I dare. Both of them are crafts, with their own set of tools, which will do the jobs they were designed to do if they are used correctly.

So I would say this to everyone who feels that his main aptitude is for science or technology, or for any other field that lies outside the humanities, and that therefore he can't write:

Learn to use the tools without fear. They are not some kind of secret apparatus owned by the English teacher or any other teacher. They are simple mechanisms for putting your thoughts on paper. Enjoy finding out how they work. Take as much pleasure in what an active verb will do for you as in what a mathematical formula will do, or a computer, or a centrifuge. The self-esteem will then take care of itself. Any time you reason your way through a complex scientific idea and put it in writing so that it's clear to somebody else, you can feel as good as Norman Mailer—and you should.

12. Worlds of Music

In 1975 when I wrote my book *On Writing Well* I had a definite model in mind—a book I hoped mine might resemble. The model, however, wasn't about writing. It was Alec Wilder's *American Popular Song,* a book about music, which had been published a year or two earlier. Ordinarily a nonfiction writer takes as his model (if he takes one at all) a work that's related to his subject. *American Popular Song* made me realize that the subject—what a book is about—isn't as important as the qualities of mind or personality that the writer brings to it.

I wasn't surprised that I liked Wilder's book. I already knew him as a composer of classical pieces and of songs like "While We're Young" that were fixtures in the repertory of cabaret singers. I had also read many interviews that caught the broad range of his musical intelligence. But the reason why his book appealed to me had far older roots. To explain why, I have to make one last trip back to my childhood—to the teacher who gave me what has been my single most enjoyable body of information.

Her name was Editha Messer, and she was the typical music teacher who came once a week to give piano lessons. Except that she wasn't typical; she had a perfect ear and she could—and would—play any kind of music. What really made her untypical, however, was that she knew when to throw away the rules of how music ought to be taught.

I was probably ten or eleven when my lessons began. They consisted of the standard pedagogical fare: Hanon's horrible scales, Diller and Quaile's dreary little children's tunes, the great composers' chestnuts like MacDowell's "To a Wild Rose," a work as hard to get rid of as the flower that it extols. I hated them all and hated having to learn and memorize them. I especially hated trying to read music. It was so much easier to ask Mrs. Messer to play the song and then try to fake it by ear.

Fakery didn't fool Editha Messer; she heard my every circumvention. But she also heard something else—a boy with a natural ear trying to disentangle himself from MacDowell's wild rose and other such strangling vines. She knew her student well, and one day she said, in effect, "You're never going to learn to read music, so I'm going to teach you the chords. Once you know the principles of harmony you'll be able to play anything you hear." She took out a little brown notebook that I can still picture and wrote out C-E-G and a few other fundamental chords in the key of C. She played them so that I could hear them and see what they looked like. Then she explained how they functioned within the key of C and in relation to the other major and minor keys. Suddenly I was in a world that I never knew existed but that seemed inevitable as soon as I heard it. Suddenly music lessons became fun. I loved how elegant the system was. Countless harmonies were waiting for me in those eighty-eight keys. All I had to do was find them.

So began a lifetime of sitting where I could watch the hands of jazz pianists and listening to their records and appropriating chords that excited me with their texture and their tension. Editha Messer had given me the tools to be my own teacher, and for a long time that sufficed—until the day at Yale when I first heard Willie Ruff's partner, Dwike Mitchell. The harmonies coming out of his piano were incredibly rich cousins of the ones I had begged, borrowed and stolen and thought were good enough. I knew it was time to go back to school, and Mitchell has been my teacher ever since.

That relationship has taught me as much about writing as it has about music. I found that the lives of Mitchell and Ruff— both as artists and as teachers—interested me on so many levels that I began to write about them, first in the *New Yorker* piece about their trip to introduce jazz to China (described in Chapter 3) and eventually in an entire book, *Willie and Dwike.* My vocation and my avocation merged—one of the best things that can happen to a writer. Writing about music also made me a better musician. The need to write clearly about an art form that the reader can never see or hear, one that evaporates with the playing of every note, forced me to think harder about the structure of music—about what I was trying to learn.

Was it possible, for instance, to convey something of what happens in a music lesson—what that transaction is like? Here's a paragraph in which I tried:

> I hear chords coming out of Mitchell's piano that make me quiver. No matter how many complex chords I already knew or have since learned, there is no end of new ones: chords that I never imagined and would never be able to find by myself. When I learn a new chord on Mitchell's piano I still can't believe that it will also exist on *my* piano, and I hurry home to try it out. But every discovery raises new questions. Having learned a chord that's exactly right for a certain song in a certain key, I'm eager to own it in every other key, and I start by transposing it up a halftone, or down, and it disappears: a shift of only half a tone has robbed it of whatever made it unique. I bring this mystery to Mitchell and he says, "That chord only works in D flat." His ear knows what every chord sounds like in every key at every register. "It's the vibrations," he says. "How the notes vibrate against each other is always

different." He talks a lot about vibrations. When he and I
analyze chords we are like two lepidopterists poring over a
tray of brilliant butterflies, delighting in their infinite variety
and their subtle gradations of color. Mitchell also talks a lot
about pressure: the pressure of the fingers on the keys. I've
begun to hear how a chord can sound wrong in any number
of ways, even when the notes are correct, and how Mitchell's
chords always sound right. He also talks about posture—the
stillness of Horowitz is a marvel to him. Most of all, he talks
about feeling. He often mentions some pianist who was technically flawless but who "might as well have not played at all."
Emotion, to him, is the crucial ingredient, and music is a total
commitment. In his conversation and his concerns I glimpse
what it is to be an artist and not just a musician.

What to play, as distinct from how to play, was never a problem: I'm a show tune addict. I got hooked at an early age when
my parents went to Cole Porter musicals like *Anything Goes*
and brought home and played the sheet music of "You're the
Top," "I Get a Kick Out of You" and other "gems from the
score." I was a small boy with three big older sisters; whatever
sophistication existed in the family stopped with them. Porter's
songs didn't turn me into Maurice Chevalier overnight. But
they opened a window into a world of "clever" grownups. I was
dazzled by Porter's lyrics—by the urbane rhymes and the continental allusions, the ironies and the languors. So *that's* what it
meant to be "sophisticated."

Soon after that, Fred Astaire put it all together for me. Six
Astaire movies rapidly came along, for which some of America's
best songwriters wrote some of their best songs: *Swing Time*
(Jerome Kern and Dorothy Fields); *Top Hat, Follow the Fleet*
and *Carefree* (Irving Berlin), and *Shall We Dance* and *Damsel
in Distress* (George and Ira Gershwin). The songs included, for
instance, Kern and Fields's "The Way You Look Tonight" and

"A Fine Romance," Berlin's "Cheek to Cheek" and "Let's Face the Music and Dance," and the Gershwins' "A Foggy Day" and "They Can't Take That Away From Me."

What inspired the writers to reach such heights was that they were writing for Astaire. They knew that nobody would ever sing those songs quite so well again, and they were right—the Brunswick records that Astaire made of the twenty-eight numbers from those films are a B.A. education in the art of writing and singing songs. Listening to them over and over, I learned from Astaire about such intangibles as timing and taste. But what anchored his achievement was his respect for the melody and the lyric—what the writers were trying to say. The result, it seemed to me, was nothing less than perfection. To this day (the songs are now on an LP album) I wouldn't want a single note or a single word of those songs to be written or sung differently.

From that launching pad I began going to Broadway musicals myself, starting with the buoyant Rodgers and Hart shows of the late thirties and early forties—shows like *Babes in Arms, Too Many Girls* and *Pal Joey,* which yielded such songs as "My Funny Valentine," "I Didn't Know What Time It Was" and "Bewitched"—and going to all the terrible Hollywood musicals for which Harold Arlen was writing a string of American classics like "Blues in the Night." After that the American musical theater turned its famous corner, generating shows whose songs actually advanced the plot or developed character, and I saw them all: Kurt Weill and Ira Gershwin's *Lady in the Dark,* Rodgers and Hammerstein's *Oklahoma!, Carousel, South Pacific* and *The King and I,* Frank Loesser's *Guys and Dolls,* Jule Styne and Stephen Sondheim's *Gypsy,* and many more.

By then I had all the earmarks of a crazed hobbyist, buying every album that reconstructed the score of a bygone show, listening to the records of such custodial singers as Frank Sinatra, Judy Garland and Ella Fitzgerald, who, like Astaire, revered these songs and sang them impeccably. As a result, the music and lyrics of at least a thousand songs from this vast American literature are cross-indexed in my brain, more instantly retrievable than any other information stored in that crowded data base.

What every collector wants, of course, is someone who shares his passion, preferably someone of greater erudition. For me that someone was Alec Wilder; *American Popular Song* was a book I had been waiting for all my life. Its theme is in its subtitle: "The Great Innovators, 1900–1950." To write his book Wilder examined the sheet music of seventeen thousand songs. From those he selected three hundred in which he felt that the composer pushed into new territory, or at least "maintained the high level of sophisticated craftsmanship" that earlier innovators had established. His focus is on the music, not the lyrics, though he cites the lyrics if necessary, and usually he also provides the music of the passage he is writing about—often just three or four measures where the composer did something he finds unusual or somehow touching. For instance, discussing George and Ira Gershwin's "A Foggy Day," Wilder writes:

It's extraordinary how constant is [George] Gershwin's use of repeated notes. They are more usually to be found in his rhythm songs, but are seldom absent, even in a tender ballad like this. For example, the very first three notes are repeated. And the notes accompanying "I viewed the" and "the British" are repeated.

In any type of song but a romantic ballad, Gershwin's angularity may produce the most effective result. But the proof that there are no hard and fast rules is "A Foggy Day." For in it there is no step-wise writing, and there are many leaps of fourth and fifth intervals. Yet it remains a most tender and moving, a far from aggressive, song.

I should make it clear that I do not view the repeated notes with alarm. "A Foggy Day," for instance, has a heartbreak quality, not one note of which would I change. Right away I am captured by the *e* flat accompanying the word "day." [The song is in the key of F.] And I am given, as a dividend, the avoidance of the cliché of the diminished chord. Instead, Gershwin uses a minor sixth chord, which is much more winning. And he remains consistent, by moving up another minor third in the melody in his second phrase, to *a* flat, and also up a fifth again at the end of the phrase.

At the end of the *B* section (the song is *A-B-A-C*), the drop to the *d* in the cadence is truly gentle and loving. It's as personal as the revelation of a secret.

This is followed by the truly chilling wedding of the word "suddenly" with the two *f*'s and the *d*.

He then winds it up by extending the last section two measures longer than is customary, in the course of which he writes a pastoral, vulnerable, childlike phrase to go with the beautifully resolving lyric.

As Ira Gershwin wrote in a different connection, who could ask for anything more? Not I. To have a musical sensibility so finely tuned analyzing three hundred finely wrought songs was as rich a gift as I could have received. Wilder had written his way down into the most minute essence of his subject—down to the individual note. It's an immensely hard kind of writing, combining a scholar's precision with an artist's wonder, and in bringing it off Wilder is both learner and teacher. As a learner he used the act of writing to capture and possess what it is about these songs that sets them apart, and in telling me what he discovered he gave me many new insights into these old friends I thought I knew so well.

But even that doesn't explain why I took *American Popular Song* as my model for *On Writing Well.* What lingered with me after reading Wilder's book was his total commitment to his enthusiasms. His book is deeply personal. It's as if he were saying, "These are some of my likes and dislikes; take 'em or leave 'em. This isn't a definitive study—it's just one man's book."

I loved the fact that it was so overwhelmingly one man's book. I loved its confidence and its prejudices. I also loved Wilder's pleasure in presenting excellence to his readers; he doesn't include poor songs in order to shoot them down. That policy connected with my own belief in not teaching by bad example. Except for a few scraps of jargon and pomposity that I put in my books to warn against the prevailing bloatage, I don't deal in junk. If writing is learned by imitation, I want every learner to imitate the best.

Thus I saw from *American Popular Song* that it might be possible to write a book about writing that would be just one man's book. I would write confidently from my own convictions and experiences—take 'em or leave 'em—and to illustrate my points I would present passages by writers I admired. Wilder's book was infinitely generous; that was worth trying to remember.

I don't mean that Wilder was a man without peeves. We wouldn't value his loves so highly if he didn't admit that certain famous songs leave him cold. He is depressed, for instance, by the "forced good cheer" of Vincent Youmans's "Rise 'n' Shine." "The injunction of 'Rise 'n' Shine' to grin and bear it," he writes, "is almost like a Christian Science recruiting song." By contrast, discussing a Howard Dietz–Arthur Schwartz number later in the book, he writes:

> "A Shine on Your Shoes" is another powerful swinger. If I'm to be cheered up, I'd prefer to try this musical accompaniment than to be exhorted to "Rise 'n' Shine." For there is wit as well as a sinewy strength to this song. And, besides, it swings; it's looser and less instructive than the other, not just lyrically, but musically.

I like the point that instructiveness in writing is a drag. If you want to preach, disguise it as entertainment. "A Shine on My Shoes," as sung by Fred Astaire in *The Bandwagon,* is an affirmation of happiness.

> The verse is extremely fine. It starts out *whap!* and never quits. In the sixth measure the singer has to practically use clarinet keys to make it. But that kind of vocal work is fun. Take a look at the "straight ahead" verve of this verse. [He provides the first eight measures.]
>
> All I need to know I'm home is this verse. But if you need more to convince you, I think the first four measures of the chorus should do it. . . .

Another crotchet of Wilder's that I liked because it took me by surprise turns up in his analysis of Berlin's "Let's Face the Music and Dance." He concedes that it's "a very well written song, that the lyric is particularly 'civilized,' that it is uncluttered, makes every point it sets out to make, indeed, deserves high praise." That's a scholar's objective judgment. But we also like our scholars to be human, and Wilder adds: "Yet I must admit to irritation in the presence of this form of minuscule melodrama. I call it Mata Hari or canoe music."

Here's an Irving Berlin song, however, that gets full devotion—in a paragraph that could apply to any of the arts in what it says about simplicity:

> "It's a Lovely Day Tomorrow" is a pure, hymn-like melody recalling Kern at his purest or Arlen in "My Shining Hour." For some it might seem just a degree too innocent to the point of being studied simplicity. I don't find it so, perhaps because I'm a musician and I know how enormously difficult it is to write a bone-simple song, within the range of an octave and employing neither artifice nor cleverness. Frankly, if this had

been the melody of "God Bless America," I'd have been far more inclined to favor it over "The Star-Spangled Banner."

*

Another kind of music that was in my ear at an early age was classical music. New York's German-Americans were long the self-appointed caretakers of Europe's musical culture in the new world, and my grandmother, Frida Zinsser, a second-generation product of that didactic tradition, saw to it that my father played the piano and the violin long after he had lost interest in those instruments and that my sisters and I got taken to Carnegie Hall and the Metropolitan Opera House. I heard the great basso Ezio Pinza as Boris Godunov long before I heard him as Emile de Becque in *South Pacific*. *"Etwas bleibt hängen,"* my grandmother would say, using the least punitive of her many German maxims, as she played Brahms and Schubert at our piano after Sunday lunch when I wanted to be out playing baseball. It means "something remains," or "something sticks," and it's as good an educational credo as I know. Many melodies and leitmotifs that are still in my head were put there by Frida Zinsser's Germanic faith in the gods of self-improvement.

Unlike listening to classical music, writing about it was a process I had never thought much about. Then I went to work for the *New York Herald Tribune* and got to know Virgil Thomson. The "Trib" in those postwar years was the best-written and best-edited newspaper in the country, and I could hardly believe my luck at being a young reporter there. We all had our desks in one room, the city room, which was as big as a city block and just as grimy. The desks were encrusted with coffee stains and the air was foul with the smell of cigarettes and cigars; during the summer it was stirred sluggishly by ancient fans with dangling electric cords that looked like the wires you see lying on the street after an ice storm. There was no air-conditioning, but we were conditioned to bad air because we were newspapermen. In the middle of the room the city editor, L. L. Engelking, a terrifying giant from Texas who was obsessed by his quest for the grail of perfection, bellowed his wrath at his imperfect help. I thought it was the most beautiful room in the world.

But there was one corner whose occupants didn't fit the journalistic image—the drama and music department. The most startling of its denizens was the legendary fop Lucius Beebe, whose column about "café society" was written in a style that was baroque, or, at the latest, rococo. Beebe came to work in a derby, attired like Beau Brummell, in raiment that except on him hadn't survived beyond Edwardian London. The next desk belonged to Walter Terry, the dance critic, who, when he stood up to stretch, often stood in Fourth Position, and beyond him sat various skittish young men and women whom the chief music critic had hired to cover the lesser concerts and recitals that *he* wouldn't be covering. One of them was the composer and writer Paul Bowles, who not long afterward moved to Tangier and never came back, perhaps driven by the squalor of the *Herald Tribune* to seek the purifying austerity of the desert, which his subsequent novels, like *The Sheltering Sky*, so vividly caught.

At the center of this small world, as oblivious of the surrounding chaos as the Buddha he slightly resembled, sat the chief critic himself—a short, somewhat round man with mirthful eyes and a look of total assurance that he belonged right where he was. Virgil Thomson was then midway through his fourteen-year reign as the preeminent music critic in America. I knew of him mainly as a composer—in particular, of *Four Saints in Three Acts*, the opera he wrote with Gertrude Stein. What I didn't know was what qualities of mind had gone into making him the preeminent music critic in America. His writing style, of course, was velvet-smooth; any reader could tell that much.

But who was *he?* I got a chance to find out in 1948 when I became drama editor of the *Herald Tribune,* responsible for the Sunday section that included theater, movies, music, dance, art and, eventually, an upstart medium called television. It was a perfect spot for Thomson-watching, and I identified three qualities that gave his work unusual strength.

First, he was fearless. During Virgil Thomson's tenure no sacred cow could safely graze. He had the most impressive enemies of any critic in town—the board members and managers who ran establishment organizations like the New York Philharmonic, which had become parochial and smug. When Artur Rodzinski resigned as the Philharmonic's conductor, alleging interference by its autocratic manager, Arthur Judson, who was also president of Columbia Concerts, a firm that sold soloists to the orchestra he was manager of, Thomson wrote a strong column condemning the conflict of interest. Judson replied that he was "now more than ever" Thomson's enemy and "would remain so." Thomson took this as good news; he said he saw it as his duty to expose the "manipulators" who controlled the musical scene and "to support with all the power of my praise every artist, composer, group or impresario whose relation to music was based only on music and the sound it makes."

To lob such a well-aimed grenade over the crenellated walls of the Philharmonic might seem satisfaction enough for one twelve-month period. But Thomson ended that same year with a scuffle that was no less piquant. Describing it some years later in his autobiography, *Virgil Thomson,* he wrote:

> In November the Pope's encyclical on art and music, *Media-tor Dei,* had been published in Rome, and our bureau chief sent it to me. It encouraged the liturgical use of modern styles in both music and art. Naturally I wrote about it, translating from an Italian text such passages as dealt specifically with

music. A flurry of querulous letters from priests editing Catholic papers hinted that the American clergy would have liked to bury the encyclical. And that is what their papers eventually did. I remembered that the American bishops had waited twenty years to implement the century's earlier encyclical about music, Pius X's *Motu Proprio,* of 1903. If now they showed a similar reluctance, that need not surprise. Nor need it stop my cheering. The Pope was news; modern music was my faith; their union was almost too good to believe.

Any critic who opens hostilities on both the New York Philharmonic and the Catholic Church in one year is not a man suffering from a failure of nerve.

Second, Virgil Thomson was no snob. Before him, chief music critics didn't stray far from their aisle seat at Carnegie Hall and the Met; they might get hit by a piece of jazz while crossing the street. Thomson's antennae were out everywhere in the American air. Here's a partial list of what he covered during his first year on the job as the *Herald Tribune*'s critic, in addition to the opera, the major orchestras and the standard soloists:

Maxine Sullivan singing in a nightclub; Paul Bowles's music for *Twelfth Night* on Broadway; Walt Disney's *Fantasia;* a student orchestra; two youth orchestras; an opera at the Juilliard School; a Bach oratorio in a church; a Broadway musical by Kurt Weill; Stravinsky's violin concerto adapted for a ballet; several other dance performances that used modern music; Holy Thursday at St. Patrick's cathedral; a black preacher in New Jersey who wore white frilled paper wings over his blue serge suit and played swing music on an electric guitar (that was the Easter Sunday piece); a WPA orchestra in Newark; a swing concert at the Museum of Modern Art; the Goldman Band in Central Park, and three suburban and regional orchestras.

That's a man who didn't put any fences around his notion of

where good or at least interesting music might be found. Moral: Think flexibly about the field you're writing about. Its frontiers may no longer be where they were last time you looked.

Finally, Thomson's style conveys great enjoyment. He's serious but never solemn; his writing has just enough irreverence to keep us off balance. Reading him, I often think: Is he really saying *that?* Here's the start of a typical Thomson review:

> Whether one is able to listen without mind-wandering to the Seventh Symphony of Dmitri Shostakovich probably depends on the rapidity of one's musical perceptions. It seems to have been written for the slow-witted, the not very musical and the distracted. In this respect it differs from nearly all those other symphonies in which abnormal length is part and parcel of the composer's concept. Beethoven's Ninth, Mahler's Ninth and Eighth, Bruckner's Seventh and the great Berlioz "machines" are long because they could not have been made any shorter without eliminating something the author wanted in. Their matter is complex and cannot be expounded briefly. The Shostakovich piece, on the other hand, is merely a stretching out of material that is in no way deep or difficult to understand.

Consider how much musical knowledge that one paragraph contains—and how entertainingly that knowledge is presented to us.

Here, in another review, Thomson dutifully pays his respects to a composer he knows he should like better than he does:

> About once a year your reviewer ventures to dip an ear again into the Wagnerian stream. He thinks he ought to find out whether anything about it has changed since the last time or if anything has possibly changed in him that might provoke a reversal of judgment about it all and a return of the passion-

ate absorption with which he used to plunge himself into that vast current of sound. . . .

The instrumentation [of *Die Walküre*] remains rich in sound and highly personal. And if it often creates its theatrical excitement by the use of mere hubbub, that excitement is still a dependable effect and the instrumental dispositions are acoustically sound. It has long seemed to me that Wagner's original contributions to musical art are chiefly of an orchestral nature. His music-writing is more varied in quality than that of any other composer of equal celebrity, even Berlioz; but no matter what the quality, it always sounds well. It is always instrumentally interesting and infallibly sumptuous. . . .

His troublesomeness on the musical scene has always been due less to the force of his musical genius than to the fact that neither instinct nor training had prepared him to criticize his own work with the objectivity that the quality of genius in it demanded. As a result, every score is a sea beach full of jewelry and jetsam. Fishing about for priceless bits is a rewarding occupation for young musicians, just as bathing in the sound of it is always agreeable to any musical ear. But musicians are likely to find nowadays that the treasure has been pretty well combed and that the continued examination of the remnants yields little they hadn't known was there before.

Like his corner of the *Herald Tribune*'s city room, Virgil Thomson's writing method didn't fit the journalistic mold. As newspapermen, the rest of us knew how things had to be done: we typed our copy, double-spaced, and made sure all the pages ended with a paragraph so they could be sent to the composing room separately after each "take" was written. Thomson would come back after a concert or an opera, remove his coat, pick up a pencil and write his review in longhand on a long yellow pad, looking as unhurried as a Victorian novelist—Trollope, per-haps—setting out to describe the English countryside, though in fact he was operating under one of the most brutal of all late-night newspaper deadlines. The sentences rolled out majestically and evidently perfectly formed, for when he reached the end of a yellow sheet, even if he was in the middle of a sentence, he called for a copy boy, who took the piece of paper and dropped it down a chute to the composing room, where a linotypist familiar with Thomson's handwriting was standing by.

I marveled at that seemingly casual act of writing, and I marveled again the next morning when I opened the paper and saw the narrative momentum with which one sentence followed another, the pertinent facts of the evening's performance so elegantly or impishly noted, the arguments for or against the performers so adroitly marshaled.

Today Virgil Thomson is ninety-one and still writing with vigor. The secret of his writing, like the secret of his music, is a hymn-like simplicity. Beneath all the graces that charm us with their civility, his writing moves, finally, with sequential logic, as all good writing must. I put him with some of my favorite stylists whose writing is unfailingly an act of clear thinking, from Thoreau and Abraham Lincoln to E. B. White and Red Smith.

*

One reason why Alec Wilder and Virgil Thomson wrote so well about other people's music is that they were composers themselves. Ultimately, however, every critic is an outsider, one step removed from the creative spark. I wondered to what extent writing could take us inside—to the process of actually making music. Could a singer write about how to sing, or a composer about what it means to compose? For an answer I turned to two great artists who are equally renowned as teachers: the soprano Phyllis Curtin and the composer Roger Sessions.

Knowing Phyllis Curtin was still another bonus of my decade at Yale. In those years she was one of the stars of the Yale School of Music; young singers came from all over the world to study voice with her. Though her own brilliant career was far from over, teaching was what nourished her most, and when she left Yale to become dean of the school of arts at Boston University it continued to be—and still is—her main fulfillment. I called her and asked whether singing, the most basic and probably most undescribable of the arts, has any accessible literature.

"Most of the books are so technical with all their talk about muscles," she said, "that you can't learn anything from them. I can only think of one book that contains the idea—the aesthetic—of what it means to be a singer. It was written by my teacher's teacher. His name was Oscar Saenger, and his book, which was called *The Oscar Saenger Course in Vocal Training*, was published in 1915 by the Victor Talking Machine Company. I doubt if there's another copy in existence, so I'll send you mine." She did, and when it came I stepped into a Victorian world. From the opening words of the preface, called "The Art of Song," I felt like singing.

Song is the noblest, the most intimate, the most complete manner of self-expression known to mankind, and in the last analysis self-expression is the great thing for which mankind is ever searching. As the power to express grows, so the higher ideals of life develop and the greatest and most subtle influences which make for culture come to have full sway.

There comes into every life a time when the inner self can no longer be reached by things from without, when the soul craves that which it can supply to itself alone. Song then becomes not only a source of forgetfulness of material things and a solace, but also an inspiration. It repays the possessor for every effort that has been lavished upon it and returns a thousandfold all that it has cost.

In a commercial age like the present we are prone to forget much that really makes life worth living. Anything which develops a love of the beautiful is of incalculable benefit to all. Song is intended to stir us into action and into a condition where we become conscious of the presence of higher, holier things than "are dreamed of in our philosophies." Rightly has the human voice been called "God's own instrument." Entrusted to the care of each human being is this instrument which, as Carlyle pointed out, has within it the power to lead us to the edge of the infinite and to enable us momentarily to gaze beyond.

As writing, that's the product of a more innocent age, but as a creed for artists it's still hard to top. Oscar Saenger's book was intended to be read in conjunction with a set of Victor records. "Learning to sing depends largely upon a student's ability to imitate," he explains, "and consequently the value of good singing records for the student can scarcely be overestimated. Imitation depends upon power of concentration and sympathetic understanding, and these qualities, so essential to the artist, may be developed rapidly by careful, conscientious *listening*."

I liked, needless to say, Saenger's emphasis on providing good models. Nowhere in his book did I feel that he was trying to be a salesman for his lessons or for Victor; the only thing he was selling was the joy of singing as well as possible. The sacred grove is opened just once to profane spirits. Realizing that he was a pioneer in home instruction by ear, he includes a short chapter called "How to Use the Victrola." "It is neither necessary nor desirable to wind the motor to its fullest possible extent," he begins. "A better way is to wind it within a few turns of the full tension and then give the winding key a few turns *between records*." That's as high as high fidelity got in 1915.

I asked Phyllis Curtin what her connection was to Oscar Saenger. "So much of what I do as a singer and as a teacher is

related to what's in that book," she told me. "My teacher was
an American basso named Joseph Regneas. He was in his eigh-
ties when I started studying with him in 1953, around the time
of my New York debut, so he must have done his own studying
with Oscar Saenger around the turn of the century. He became
such an avid disciple that he changed his name, which actually
was Joseph Baernstein, to Regneas, which is Saenger spelled
backward. What he learned from Saenger must have had a
powerful influence on his concept of tone, for at least half a
dozen times in my career i've had a singer or a vocal coach
come up to me after a concert and say, 'I've only heard a tone
floated like that by one other singer,' and in every case the other
singer had been a student of Joseph Regneas."

One of those tone detectives once asked Phyllis Curtin
whether she knew Oscar Saenger's book. She didn't, so he sent
her his copy. "As soon as I looked into it," she said, "it was so
familiar to me in all its principles."

Looking into Saenger's book myself, I was struck not only by
the clarity of its instruction, but by its insistence that mechani-
cal proficiency in a singer is never enough:

> The tone should be made to focus on the back of the upper
> front teeth and the hard palate (roof of the mouth). As an
> illustration: Close your lips and try to sing the letter *M*. A
> distinct vibration will be felt in the region of the hard palate
> and the front teeth. That is the point on which most tones
> should be focused. In the case of the head tones the point of
> focus rises until, in the extreme high register, the sensation is
> that of placing the tone high in the head.

> It is a matter of sensation and mental concentration. The
> way to place the tone forward is to *think* it forward. That is
> actually the way in which the student must focus her tone. She
> must *think* it into place and put it there through the exercise
> of a purely mental process.

At that sentence I heard the connection between Phyllis Curtin and Oscar Saenger's book click into place. I remembered
auditing one of her master classes at Yale, in which she warned
her students that technique would take them only so far and
exhorted them to be true to their individuality. "Singing," she
said, "is an impulse to move. If your mind is only on pushing the
button, there isn't any singing. You have to keep putting the
thought in front of the tone. You have to have something that
you want to say."

*

Of all the mysteries in music, none is more profound than the
mystery of composition. Still, like other abstruse disciplines—
philosophy, for example, or religion—it can be written about.
The following passage by Roger Sessions reduces a complex
intellectual act to terms that are disarmingly simple. I've chosen it because for more than half a century Sessions, who died
in 1985, at the age of eighty-nine, was not only one of America's
most prolific and adventurous composers. He was also an influential teacher, mainly at Princeton and at Berkeley, and this
final chapter of *Writing to Learn,* though ostensibly about
music, is equally—music being dependent for its nurture on
men and women in every generation who freely pass along
what they know—a chapter about teachers.

In trying to understand the work of the composer, one must
first think of him as living in a world of sounds, which in
response to his creative impulse become animated with movement. The first stage in his work is that of what is generally
known by the somewhat shopworn and certainly unscientific
term "inspiration." The composer, to use popular language
again, "has an idea"—an idea consisting of definite musical
notes and rhythms, which will engender for him the momentum with which his musical thought proceeds. The inspiration

may come in a flash, or, as sometimes happens, it may grow and develop gradually. I have in my possession photostatic copies of several pages of Beethoven's sketches for the last movement of his "Hammerklavier Sonata"; the sketches show him carefully modeling, then testing in systematic and apparently cold-blooded fashion, the theme of the fugue. Where, one might ask, is the inspiration here? Yet if the word has any meaning at all, it is certainly appropriate to this movement, with its irresistible and titanic energy of expression, already present in the theme. The inspiration takes the form, however, not of a sudden flash of music, but of a clearly-envisaged impulse toward a certain goal for which the composer was obliged to strive. When this perfection was attained, however, there could have been no hesitation—rather a flash of recognition that this was exactly what he wanted.

For any music lover that paragraph is a treat—the composer Sessions putting himself inside the head of the composer Beethoven. (For any writer it's also a crash course in rewriting.) There's no trace of pedantry in the style; Sessions conveys his excitement over Beethoven's achievement by using the tools of good English. "Titanic energy" says it all about Beethoven.

After "inspiration," Sessions goes on to explain, the composer's principal problem is to recapture that inspiration in every phase of his work—to bring "the requisite amount of energy to bear on every detail, as well as, constantly, on his vision of the whole." This vision of the whole is the "conception." That brings Sessions to the third pillar of the composer's edifice—the "execution":

The process of execution is first of all that of listening inwardly to the music as it shapes itself; of allowing the music to grow; of following both inspiration and conception wherever they may lead. A phrase, a motif, a rhythm, even a chord, may contain within itself, in the composer's imagination, the energy which produces movement. It will lead the composer on, through the force of its own momentum or tension, to other phrases, other motifs, other chords.

Continuing to lead us through these compositional steps, in language that is vivid and concrete, Sessions comes at last to the mystery that lies at the heart of the creative process, not just in music but in writing, painting, sculpture and every other art, as well as in mathematics, the sciences and the humanities. The mathematician, the scientist and the philosopher, thinking and writing their way toward the center of a problem, are no less immersed than the composer, the artist and the writer in an act of commitment that they can never recover or even explain. What finally impels them all is not the work they achieve, but the work of achieving it.

That act of commitment and discovery in every area of knowledge is the essence of this book, and I'm happy to let Roger Sessions sum it up for me and see you to the door:

How far is the composer "conscious" while he is composing? Of what is he thinking, what are his feelings? The answer, I think, is that composition is a *deed*, an action, and a genuine action of any kind is, psychologically speaking, the simplest thing in the world. Is not its subjective essence intentness on the deed? The climber in the high mountains is intent on the steps he is taking, on the practical realization of those steps; if he allows his consciousness to dwell even on their implications, his foot may move the fatal half inch too far in the direction of the abyss at his side. The composer working at his music is faced with no such tragic alternatives; but his psychology is not dissimilar. He is not so much conscious of his ideas as possessed by them. Very often he is unaware of his exact processes of thought till he is through with them; extremely often the completed work is incomprehensible to him immediately after it is finished.

Why? Because his experience in creating the work is incalculably more intense than any later experience he can have from it; because the finished product is the goal of that experience and not in any sense a repetition of it. He cannot relive the experience without effort which seems quite irrelevant. And yet he is too close to it to detach himself to the extent necessary to see his work objectively and to allow it to exert its inherent power over him.

For this reason I have always profoundly disagreed with the definition made by one of my most distinguished living colleagues who, elaborating Aristotle's famous definition of art, wrote that art on the highest level is concerned with *"der Wiedergabe der inneren Natur"*—literally translated, the reproduction of inner nature. It seems to me, on the contrary, that art is a function, an activity of the inner nature—that the artist's effort is, using the raw and undisciplined materials with which his inner nature provides him, to endow them with a meaning which they do not of themselves possess—to transcend them by giving them artistic form.

Acknowledgments

Many people have put some part of themselves into this book, and I'm grateful to them all for their time and their ideas. I particularly want to thank:

• Professor Thomas Gover of Gustavus Adolphus College, whose telephone call started it all and whose hospitality on my two trips to Minnesota was the push that kept me going; and the many men and women of the Gustavus Adolphus faculty who told me in such helpful detail about their experiences as teachers of "W" courses.

• Al Silverman, chairman of the Book-of-the-Month Club, who, during my eight years in his employment, never complained about—and, on the contrary, encouraged—my periodic jaunts to colleges, schools and teachers' conferences. Many of the ideas in this book grew out of conversations I had with the people I met on those trips.

• Terry Karten of Harper & Row, who first focused my mind on the fact that writing is an important component of learning—a point I somehow hadn't focused on before—and thereby gave this book its deeper theme and, indirectly, its title; and Buz Wyeth, my editor-in-chief at Harper & Row, who, in a relationship that goes back more than twenty years, has been unfailingly supportive of my work.

• John S. Rosenberg, a one-time writing student of mine at

Yale, who has generously gone over the manuscripts of my last four books, at my request, for matters of structure, substance and tone. He edited this book as it was being written, giving me wise course corrections for later chapters, and again when it was finished. My definition of a good editor is someone whose suggestions are always valid, whether or not the writer decides to accept them. John Rosenberg fits that definition, and I usually take his advice. He knows what I'm trying to do and knows when I'm not doing it.

The following professors freely donated valuable time and ideas: Kai Erikson, Edmund S. Morgan, Keith Stewart Thomson and the late Brand Blanshard of Yale; Monte Wilson of Boise State University; Maxine Hairston of the University of Texas; Lawrence W. Potts of Gustavus Adolphus College, and Dennis M. Read of Denison University.

The following friends and colleagues steered me to writers I wouldn't have known about or made some other contribution that I gratefully used: William B. Carlin, the late Eugene Cook, Nathan Garland, Martin Goldman, Corby Kummer, Larry Shapiro, Alan Siegel, Joel Vance, and, finally, Caroline Zinsser, my wife, who knows far more about teaching and learning than I ever will.

Sources and Notes

In this section I have mainly cited the original hardcover edition, but often the book has also become available in paperback. I want to thank the writers, editors, publishers and agents who gave me permission to reprint these passages.

Chapter 3: A Liberal Education

PAGE

27   After graduation Michael Poliakoff became a professor of classics.

30   "Shanghai Blues," by William Zinsser, *The New Yorker*, Sept. 21, 1981. Also in *Willie and Dwike: An American Profile,* by William Zinsser. Harper & Row, 1984.

32   What Ruff's tape recorder heard that night in Venice is available on a record. "Willie Ruff Solo French Horn: Gregorian Chant, Plain Chant and Spirituals." Kepler Records, P.O. Box 1779, New Haven, CT 06507.

33   "Resonance," *The New Yorker*, April 23, 1984. Also in *Willie and Dwike.*

36   Edmund S. Morgan, *The Birth of the Republic.* University of Chicago Press, 1956, 1977.

37   David F. Musto, "As American as Apple Pie," *Yale Alumni Magazine,* January 1972.

PAGE
38　"Iatrogenic Addiction: The Problem, Its Definition and History" (Musto), *Bulletin of the New York Academy of Medicine*, Second series, Vol. 61, No. 8, October 1985.

41　Brand Blanshard, *On Philosophical Style*. Greenwood Press, 1969.

Chapter 4: Writing to Learn

53　One unspoken obstacle to a broader-based teaching of writing in American colleges is a tendency in many English departments to regard writing teachers as second-class citizens. The politics of Academia is not the province of this book; the battle will have to be fought from within. A bracing call to arms in these "Mandarin Wars" was sounded by Maxine Hairston, Professor of English at the University of Texas at Austin, in her Chair's address to the annual convention of the Conference on College Composition and Communication in 1985.

"Our experience [as writing teachers] is much like that of the women's movement," Professor Hairston said. "One can look at how far we have come and rejoice at our progress, or one can look at the barriers that still exist and become discouraged. A major reason we get discouraged is that our major problems originate close to home: in our own departments and within the discipline of English studies itself. And we are having trouble solving those problems precisely because they are so immediate and daily, and because we have complex psychological bonds to the people who so frequently are our adversaries in our efforts to make the writing programs in our departments as good as they should be and can be.

"I think the time has come to break those bonds. . . . As rhetoricians and writing teachers we will come of age and become autonomous professionals with a discipline of our own only if we can make a psychological break with the literary critics who today dominate the profession of English studies. Until we move out from behind their shadows and no longer accept their definition of what our profession should be, we are not going to have full confidence in our own mission and our own professionalism. . . . But logic has long since ceased to be a consideration in this dispute. For the literary establishment, the issue is power; they do not want to relinquish their control of all of English. For us, the issue is survival. We must cut our psychological ties in order to mature." *College Composition and Communication,* Vol. XXXVI, No. 3, October 1985. National Council of Teachers of English, 1111 Kenyon Road, Urbana, IL 61801.

Chapter 5: Crotchets and Convictions

55 Paul Klee's painting on the jacket of this book is called "Mural from the Temple of Longing: Thither." I felt that Klee was the artist who would come closest to "illustrating" what *Writing to Learn* is about.

56 An article that helped me to think about various "types" of writing and how they frequently overlap—a thoughtful exploration of the subject—is Maxine Hairston's "Different Products, Different Processes: A Theory About Writing," *College Composition and Communication,* Vol. XXXVII, No. 4, December 1986. (See above.)

58 *Grammatical Man: Information, Entropy, Language, and Life,* by Jeremy Campbell. Simon & Schuster, 1952.

62 *Pluto's Republic* (incorporating *The Art of the Soluble* and *Induction and Intuition in Scientific Thought*), by Peter Medawar. Oxford University Press, 1982 (paperback). Medawar died in 1987.

63 *The Elements of Style,* by William Strunk, Jr., and E. B.

PAGE

White. Macmillan Publishing Company, 1959; paper-back, 1972.

71   The Orwell passage is from his famous essay, "Politics and the English Language," an attack on the use of obfuscation by rulers to hide unpleasant truths from the populace. "In our time," he writes, "political speech and writing are largely the defense of the indefensible. Thus political language has to consist largely of euphemism, question-begging and sheer cloudy vagueness."

71   "The Death of Benny Paret," from *The Presidential Papers,* by Norman Mailer. Reprinted by permission of the author and the author's agents, Scott Meredith Literary Agency, Inc., 845 Third Avenue, New York, NY 10022.

73   "On Being Ill," from *The Moment and Other Essays,* by Virginia Woolf. Copyright 1945 by Harcourt Brace Jovanovich, Inc.; renewed 1976 by Harcourt Brace Jovanovich, Inc., and Marjorie T. Parsons. Reprinted by permission of the publisher.

74   *Mountbatten,* by Philip Ziegler. Alfred A. Knopf, Inc., 1985.

Chapter 6: Earth, Sea and Sky

81   "The Life History of a Mountain Range—The Appalachians," by John Rodgers, from *Mountain Building Processes,* edited by K.J. Shü. Academic Press, 1982.

82   "The Geological History of Connecticut," by John Rodgers, from *Discovery,* The Peabody Museum, Yale University, Vol. 15, No. 1, 1980. Copyright © Yale Peabody Museum of Natural History.

85   *Meditations at 10,000 Feet: A Scientist in the Mountains,* by James Trefil. Charles Scribner's Sons, an imprint of Macmillan Publishing Company, 1986.

PAGE

88 "The Catastrophic Late Pleistocene Bonneville Flood in the Snake River Plain, Utah," by Harold E. Malde. Geological Professional Paper 596, Department of the Interior, United States Government Printing Office, 1968.

89 "The Earthquake," by John Muir, from *The Wilderness World of John Muir,* edited by Edwin Way Teale. Houghton Mifflin Co., 1954. Originally published in Houghton Mifflin's *Our National Parks.*

92 *Cry, the Beloved Country,* by Alan Paton. Charles Scribner's Sons, 1948.

93 From *A Sand County Almanac: And Sketches Here and There* by Aldo Leopold. Copyright 1949, 1977 by Oxford University Press, Inc. Reprinted by permission.

95 "Slip-Sliding Away," by Ed Marston and Mary Moran, from *High Country News,* June 9, 1986. Box 1090, Paonia, Colorado 81428.

97 From *The Sea Around Us,* Revised Edition, by Rachel Carson. Copyright © 1950, 1951, 1961 by Rachel L. Carson; renewed 1979 by Roger Christie. Reprinted by permission of Oxford University Press, Inc.

100 *Meditations at 10,000 Feet,* by James Trefil. Cited above.

Chapter 7: Art and Artists

104 At George Nelson's memorial service in 1986, one former client spoke of the freshness of his thinking in 1940; another recalled the freshness of his thinking in 1986, the year he died. Noting this fact in a memoir in the magazine *ID,* the critic Ralph Caplan said: "A recent study of disorientation and memory loss among the elderly reports that people can be helped by simple exer-

PAGE

cises requiring them to think. The problem is not so much deterioration as the loss of what might be called the habit of thinking. It was a habit George Nelson never gave up, and his persistence in thinking as a design function was at the heart of his effectiveness as a design consultant."

104   *How to See: Visual Adventures in a World God Never Made,* by George Nelson. Copyright © 1977 by George Nelson. By permission of Little, Brown and Company.

106   *Meanings of Modern Art,* by John Russell. Copyright © 1981 by John Russell. Reprinted by permission of Harper & Row, Publishers, Inc.

110   "An Earthwork Looks at the Sky," by John Russell. From the *New York Times,* January 5, 1986. Copyright © 1986 by the New York Times Company. Reprinted by permission.

112   *Prints & People: A Social History of Printed Pictures,* by A. Hyatt Mayor. New York Graphic Society (Little, Brown and Company), 1972.

113   *Prints & People.*

115   *Looking at Photographs: 100 Pictures from the Collection of the Museum of Modern Art,* by John Szarkowski. New York Graphic Society (Little, Brown and Company), 1973.

116   *Looking at Photographs.*

118   *Paul Rand: A Designer's Art,* by Paul Rand. Yale University Press, 1985.

120   "On the Choice of Typefaces," from *The Crystal Goblet: Sixteen Essays on Typography,* by Beatrice Warde. World Publishing Company, 1956.

121   *The Art of Seeing,* by Aldous Huxley. Montana Books,

Publishers, Inc., 1975. Originally published by Harper & Row.

122 *Art and Illusion: A Study in the Psychology of Pictorial Representation,* by E. H. Gombrich. Published by Phaidon Press, 1959.

Chapter 8: The Natural World

127 *So Excellent a Fishe: A Natural History of Sea Turtles,* by Archie Carr. Natural History Press, 1967. Reprinted by permission of Doubleday & Company.

130 *So Excellent a Fishe.*

131 *The Voyage of the Beagle,* by Charles Darwin. Anchor Books paperback, Doubleday & Company.

136 "Missouri's Water Snakes . . . A Closer Look," by Tom R. Johnson, from *Missouri Conservationist,* June 1987. Copyright © by the Conservation Commission of the State of Missouri, P.O. Box 180, Jefferson City, MO 65102. Reprinted with permission.

140 *The Insect World of J. Henri Fabre,* edited with introduction and interpretive comments by Edwin Way Teale. Reprinted by permission of Dodd, Mead & Company, Inc.

144 *Speak, Memory,* by Vladimir Nabokov. Copyright © 1960, 1966 by Vladimir Nabokov. G. P. Putnam's Sons.

145 *Birds and Their Attributes,* by Glover Morrill Allen. Marshall Jones Company, 1925. Dover paperback, 1962.

Chapter 9: Writing Mathematics

158 The problem about population growth and bacterial growth is from "The Exponential Function: A Problem-

Centered Approach," a paper by Mel Griffith, Tony Sedgwick and Tom Seidenberg, presented at the Woodrow Wilson Institute's Mathematics Institute, summer 1985.

160 The "very surprising" result of the China problem was that there would be no difference in the proportion of girls and boys in the Chinese population.

167 Two books recommended by Joan Countryman for clear writing on mathematics are *The Mathematical Experience,* by Philip J. Davis and Reuben Hersh, Houghton Mifflin Co., 1981, and *Descartes' Dream: The World According to Mathematics,* by the same authors, Harcourt Brace Jovanovich, 1986. A book that took me enjoyably and painlessly into the mind and the life work of a great mathematician is S. M. Ulam's *Adventures of a Mathematician* (Scribner paperback). Several teachers have spoken admiringly of Alfred North Whitehead's *Introduction to Mathematics.* Professor Keith Stewart Thomson of Yale, former dean of the Yale Graduate School, told me: "I would recommend any part, but especially the first two chapters, of Whitehead's book. His style is perfect for his purpose—to talk about mathematics without scaring the reader."

Chapter 10: Man, Woman and Child

168 *Extraordinary Lives: The Art and Craft of Biography,* American Heritage, 1986. *Spiritual Quests: The Art and Craft of Religious Writing,* Houghton Mifflin, 1988.

173 "A Long Line of Cells," by Lewis Thomas, from *Inventing the Truth: The Art and Craft of Memoir.* Houghton Mifflin Co., 1987. Copyright © 1986 by Lewis Thomas.

174 "Dancers of Bali: Gamelan Orchestra from the Village of Pliatan, Indonesia," Columbia Records ML 4618. This

LP album made by Columbia Records during the Broadway run of the Balinese troupe may still be in the bins of historically-minded record stores.

175 *Growing Up in New Guinea: A Comparative Study of Primitive Education,* by Margaret Mead. Copyright © 1930, 1958, 1962 by Margaret Mead. Reprinted by permission of William Morrow & Co.

178 "Deep Play: Notes on the Balinese Cockfight," from *The Interpretation of Cultures,* by Clifford Geertz. Basic Books, 1973. Originally published in *Daedalus,* Vol. 100, No. 1 ("Myth, Symbol and Culture"), Winter 1972. Reprinted by permission of *Daedalus,* Journal of the American Academy of Arts and Sciences, Boston, MA.

184 *The Hidden Dimension,* by Edward T. Hall. Doubleday & Company, 1966.

188 *Children of Crisis,* Vol. 1, "A Study of Courage and Fear," by Robert Coles. Copyright © 1964, 1965, 1966, 1967 by Robert Coles. By permission of Little, Brown and Company in association with the Atlantic Monthly Press.

Chapter 11: Writing Physics and Chemistry

192 *Relativity: The Special and the General Theory,* by Albert Einstein, translation by Robert W. Lawson. © MCMLXI by The Estate of Albert Einstein. Used by permission of Crown Publishers, Inc.

198 On the study of physics: I. I. Rabi, one of the most revered and influential of twentieth-century physicists, died on January 11, 1988, at the age of eighty-nine. His obituary in the *New York Times* said that Dr. Rabi considered physics "the most ennobling of disciplines, as well as the most fundamental," and that he always tried to impart

to his students a sense of its greatness. "You're wrestling with a champ," he told them. "You're trying to find out how God made the world, just like Jacob wrestling with the angel."

198   On translation: The preceding passages by Albert Einstein, translated from the German, and the following passages by Primo Levi, translated from the Italian, further illustrate the point about translation made in Chapter 8 (page 139) in connection with the prose of the French entomologist J. Henri Fabre: that writing which is orderly in structure and precise in detail will usually survive—as it should—the perils of crossing into another language.

198   Primo Levi's Auschwitz books are *Survival in Auschwitz* (1947), *The Reawakening* (1963) and *The Drowned and the Saved* (1988).

199   *The Periodic Table,* by Primo Levi. Translated by Raymond Rosenthal. Translation copyright © 1984 by Schocken Books. Reprinted by permission of Schocken Books, published by Pantheon Books, a division of Random House, Inc.

203   "Requiring Good Writing in Chemistry Courses," by Estelle K. Meislich, from *The Journal of Chemical Education,* Volume 64, no. 6, June 1987. University of Texas, Austin, Texas 78712.

206   "Critical-Thinking Writing Assignments in General Chemistry," by Naola VanOrden, from *The Journal of Chemical Education,* same issue.

Chapter 12: Worlds of Music

213   *Willie and Dwike,* by William Zinsser.
215   The Astaire album is called "Starring Fred Astaire." Columbia Records.

PAGE

216   From *American Popular Song: The Great Innovators
      1900–1950* by Alec Wilder. Copyright © 1972 by Alec
      Wilder and James T. Maher. Reprinted by permission of
      Oxford University Press, Inc.

222   *Virgil Thomson,* by Virgil Thomson. Alfred A. Knopf,
      Inc., 1966.

224   *The Musical Scene* (Collected Reviews and Columns), by
      Virgil Thomson. Alfred A. Knopf, Inc., 1945.

227   *The Oscar Saenger Course in Vocal Training,* by Oscar
      Saenger. Victor Talking Machine Company, 1915.

229   Re Joseph Regneas: My new year's wish for Phyllis Cur-
      tin, I told her, was that one of her students would be so
      influenced by her teaching that she would change her
      last name to Nitruc.

230   *Roger Sessions on Music: Collected Essays,* by Roger Ses-
      sions, edited by Edward T. Cone. Copyright © 1979 by
      Princeton University Press. (Originally published in *The
      Intent of the Artist,* by S. Anderson et al., Augusto Cen-
      teno, editor. Copyright © 1941, © 1969 renewed by
      Princeton University Press.) Reprinted by permission of
      Princeton University Press.

Index

There's an epidemic with 27 million victims. And no visible symptoms.

It's an epidemic of people who can't read.

Believe it or not, 27 million Americans are functionally illiterate, about one adult in five.

The solution to this problem is you... when you join the fight against illiteracy. So call the Coalition for Literacy at toll-free **1-800-228-8813** and volunteer.

**Volunteer
Against Illiteracy.
The only degree you need
is a degree of caring.**

Ad Council Coalition for Literacy